HARD QUESTIONS, REAL ANSWERS

HARD QUESTIONS, REAL ANSWERS

William Lane Craig

CROSSWAY BOOKS

A DIVISION OF
GOOD NEWS PUBLISHERS
WHEATON, ILLINOIS

Hard Questions, Real Answers

Copyright © 2003 by William Lane Craig

Published by Crossway Books
        a division of Good News Publishers
        1300 Crescent Street
        Wheaton, Illinois 60187

Portions of the introduction, chapters 1–5, and chapter 8 were previously published as *No Easy Answers* (Chicago: Moody, 1990).

Cover design: Josh Dennis

First printing 2003

Printed in the United States of America

Library of Congress Cataloging-in-Publication Data
Craig, William Lane.
   Hard questions, real answers / William Lane Craig.
     p. cm.
   "Portions of the introduction, chapters 1-5, and chapter 8 were previously published as No easy answers"—T.p. verso.
   Includes bibliographical references and index.
   ISBN 1-58134-487-2 (pbk.)
   1. Apologetics. I. Craig, William Lane. No easy answers. II. Title.
BT1103.C73   2003
239—dc22   2003017935

BP		13	12	11	10	09	08	07	06	05	04	03
15	14	13	12	11	10	9	8	7	6	5	4	3	2	1

CONTENTS

PREFACE

This book is a revised and expanded version of my earlier book *No Easy Answers*. The original book flowed out of a series of sermons I delivered on "Unpopular Themes," that is, topics frequently shunned because of the hard questions they raise. As a Christian philosopher and theologian, I have been impressed at how much easier it is to raise hard questions than to answer them. Students and laymen who have little philosophical or theological training sometimes pose difficult questions which are even knottier than they themselves realize. They deserve better than pat answers. They deserve real answers, which is what I try to give in this book.

I've tried to preserve in this book something of the informal, oral style of the sermons that inspired it. I offered the original as a book more devotional in orientation than academic, but I fear that most folks found it hopelessly cerebral. I guess that for those of us for whom the life of the mind is important, our devotional lives are inextricably intertwined with our intellectual lives. But that's okay. We're commanded to love the Lord with all our hearts and with all our minds. I hope that readers who have been struggling with some of the hard questions will find this multifaceted love of the Lord kindled afresh within them.

—William Lane Craig
Atlanta, Georgia
August 2003

INTRODUCTION

IN INTELLECTUAL NEUTRAL

A number of years ago, two books appeared that sent shock waves through the American educational community. The first of these, *Cultural Literacy: What Every American Needs to Know,* by E. D. Hirsch, documented the fact that large numbers of American college students do not have the basic background knowledge to understand the front page of a newspaper or to act responsibly as citizens. For example, a quarter of the students in a recent survey thought Franklin D. Roosevelt was president during the Vietnam War. Two-thirds did not know when the Civil War occurred. One-third thought Columbus discovered the New World sometime after 1750. In a recent survey at California State University at Fullerton, over half of the students could not identify Chaucer or Dante. Ninety percent did not know who Alexander Hamilton was, despite the fact that his picture is on every ten dollar bill.

These statistics would be funny if they weren't so alarming. What has happened to our schools that they should be producing such dreadfully ignorant people? Allan Bloom, who was an eminent educator at the University of Chicago and the author of the second book I referred to above, argued in *The Closing of the American Mind* that behind the current educational malaise lies the universal conviction of students that all truth is relative and, therefore, that truth is not worth pursuing. Bloom writes,

There is one thing a professor can be absolutely certain of: almost every student entering the university believes, or says he believes, that truth is relative. If this belief is put to the test, one can count on the students' reaction: they will be uncomprehending. That anyone should regard the proposition as not self-evident astonishes them, as though he were calling into question $2 + 2 = 4$. These are things you don't think about. . . . That it is a moral issue for students is revealed by the character of their response when challenged—a combination of disbelief and indignation: "Are you an absolutist?," the only alternative they know, uttered in the same tone as . . . "Do you really believe in witches?" This latter leads into the indignation, for someone who believes in witches might well be a witch-hunter or a Salem judge. The danger they have been taught to fear from absolutism is not error but intolerance. Relativism is necessary to openness; and this is the virtue, the only virtue, which all primary education for more than fifty years has dedicated itself to inculcating. Openness—and the relativism that makes it the only plausible stance in the face of various claims to truth and various ways of life and kinds of human beings—is the great insight of our times. . . . The study of history and of culture teaches that all the world was mad in the past; men always thought they were right, and that led to wars, persecutions, slavery, xenophobia, racism, and chauvinism. The point is not to correct the mistakes and really be right; rather it is not to think you are right at all.[1]

Since there is no absolute truth, since everything is relative, the purpose of an education is not to learn truth or master facts—rather it is merely to acquire a skill so that one can go out and obtain wealth, power, and fame. Truth has become irrelevant.

Now, of course, this sort of relativistic attitude toward truth is antithetical to the Christian worldview. For as Christians we believe that all truth is God's truth, that God has revealed to us the truth, both in His Word and in Him who said, "I am the Truth." The Christian, therefore, can never look on the truth with apathy or disdain. Rather, he cherishes and treasures the truth as a reflection of God Himself. Nor does his commitment to truth make the Christian intolerant, as Bloom's students erroneously inferred; on the contrary, the very

---

[1] Allan Bloom, *The Closing of the American Mind* (New York: Simon & Schuster, 1987), 25-26.

concept of tolerance entails that one does not agree with that which one tolerates. The Christian is committed to both truth and tolerance, for he believes in Him who said not only, "I am the Truth," but also, "Love your enemies."

At the time that these books were released, I was teaching in the Religious Studies department at a Christian liberal arts college. So I began to wonder: how much have Christian students been infected with the attitude that Bloom describes? How would my own students fare on one of E. D. Hirsch's tests? *Well, how would they?* I thought. *Why not give them a quiz?* So I did.

I drew up a brief, general knowledge quiz about famous people, places, and things and administered it to two classes of about fifty sophomores. What I found was that although they did better than the general student population, still there were sizable portions of the group who could not identify—even with a phrase—some important names and events. For example, 49 percent could not identify Leo Tolstoy, the author of perhaps the world's greatest novel, *War and Peace*. To my surprise, 16 percent did not know who Winston Churchill was. One student thought he was one of the founding fathers of our nation! Another identified him as a great revival preacher of a few hundred years ago! Twenty-two percent did not know what Afghanistan is, and 22 percent could not identify Nicaragua. Twenty percent did not know where the Amazon River is. Imagine!

They fared even worse with things and events. I was amazed that a whopping 67 percent could not identify the Battle of the Bulge. Several identified it as a dieter's problem. Twenty-four percent did not know what the Special Theory of Relativity is (mind you, just to identify it—even as, say, "a theory of Einstein"—not to explain it). Forty-five percent couldn't identify Custer's Last Stand—it was variously classed as a battle in the Revolutionary War or as a battle in the Civil War. And I wasn't really surprised that 73 percent did not know what the expression "manifest destiny" referred to.

So it became clear to me that Christian students have not been able to rise above the dark undertow in our educational system at the primary and secondary levels. This level of ignorance presents a real crisis for Christian colleges and seminaries.

But then an even more terrible fear began to dawn on me as I contemplated these statistics. *If Christian students are this ignorant of the general facts of history and geography,* I thought, *then the chances are that they, and Christians in general, are equally or even more ignorant of the facts of our own Christian heritage and doctrine.* Our culture in general has sunk to the level of biblical and theological illiteracy. A great many, if not most, people cannot even name the four Gospels—in a recent survey one person identified them as Matthew, Mark, and Luther! In another survey, Joan of Arc was identified by some as Noah's wife! The suspicion arose in my mind that the evangelical church is probably also caught somewhere higher up in this same downward spiral.

But if we do not preserve the truth of our own Christian heritage and doctrine, who will learn it for us? Non-Christians? That hardly seems likely. If the Church does not treasure her own Christian truth, then it will be lost to her forever. So how, I wondered, would Christians fare on a quiz over general facts of Christian history and doctrine?

Well, how would they? I now invite you to get out a pen and paper and take the following quiz yourself. (Go on, it'll only take a minute!) The following are items I think any mature Christian in our society ought to be able to identify. Simply provide some identifying phrase that indicates that you know what the item is. For example, if I say, "John Wesley," you might write: "the founder of Methodism" or "an eighteenth-century English revivalist."

Quiz
1. Augustine
2. Council of Nicea
3. Trinity
4. Two natures united in one person
5. Pantheism
6. Thomas Aquinas
7. Reformation
8. Martin Luther

9. Substitutionary atonement
10. Enlightenment

How did you do? If you're typical of the audiences to whom I've given this quiz, probably not too well. If that is the case, you might be tempted to react to this quiz defensively: "Who needs to know all this stuff anyway? I'm not on 'Who Wants to be a Millionaire?'! This junk isn't important. All that really counts is my walk with Christ and my sharing Him with others. Who cares about all this other trivia?"

I truly hope that will not be your reaction, for that will close you off to self-improvement, and this little exercise will have been of no profit to you. You will have learned nothing from it.

But there's a second, more positive reaction. You may see, perhaps for the first time in your life, that here is a need in your life for you to become intellectually engaged as a Christian, and you may resolve to do something about it. This is a momentous decision. You will be taking a step that millions of Christians in the United States need to take. No one has issued a more forceful challenge to Christians to become intellectually engaged than did Charles Malik, former Lebanese ambassador to the United States, in his address at the dedication of the Billy Graham Center in Wheaton, Illinois. Malik emphasized that as Christians we face two tasks in our evangelism: saving the soul and saving the mind, that is to say, not only converting people spiritually, but converting them intellectually as well. And the Church is lagging dangerously behind with regard to this second task. Our churches are filled with people who are spiritually born again, but who still think like non-Christians. Mark his words well:

> I must be frank with you: the greatest danger confronting American evangelical Christianity is the danger of anti-intellectualism. The mind in its greatest and deepest reaches is not cared for enough. But intellectual nurture cannot take place apart from profound immersion for a period of years in the history of thought and the spirit. People who are in a hurry to get out of the university and start earn-

ing money or serving the church or preaching the gospel have no idea of the infinite value of spending years of leisure conversing with the greatest minds and souls of the past, ripening and sharpening and enlarging their powers of thinking. The result is that the arena of creative thinking is vacated and abdicated to the enemy.[2]

Malik went on to say:

It will take a different spirit altogether to overcome this great danger of anti-intellectualism. For example, I say this different spirit, so far as philosophy alone—the most important domain for thought and intellect—is concerned, must see the tremendous value of spending an entire year doing nothing but poring intensely over the *Republic* or the *Sophist* of Plato, or two years over the *Metaphysics* or the *Ethics* of Aristotle, or three years over the *City of God* of Augustine. But if a start is made now on a crash program in this and other domains, it will take at least a century to catch up with the Harvards and Tübingens and the Sorbonnes—and by then where will these universities be?[3]

What Malik clearly saw is the strategic position occupied by the university in shaping Western thought and culture. Indeed, the single most important institution shaping Western society is the university. It is at the university that our future political leaders, our journalists, our lawyers, our teachers, our scientists, our business executives, our artists, will be trained. It is at the university that they will formulate or, more likely, simply absorb the worldview that will shape their lives. And since these are the opinion-makers and leaders who shape our culture, the worldview that they imbibe at the university will be the one that shapes our culture.

Why is this important? Simply because the gospel is never heard in isolation. It is always heard against the background of the cultural milieu in which one lives. A person raised in a cultural milieu in which Christianity is still seen as an intellectually viable option will

[2] Charles Malik, "The Other Side of Evangelism," *Christianity Today,* November 7, 1980, 40.
[3] Ibid.

display an openness to the gospel which a person who is secularized will not display. For the secular person you may as well tell him to believe in fairies or leprechauns as in Jesus Christ! Or, to give a more realistic illustration, it is like a devotee of the Hare Krishna movement approaching you on the street and inviting you to believe in Krishna. Such an invitation strikes us as bizarre, freakish, even amusing. But to a person on the streets of Bombay, such an invitation would, I assume, appear quite reasonable and cause for reflection. I fear that evangelicals appear almost as weird to persons on the streets of Bonn, Stockholm, or Toronto as do the devotees of Krishna.

It is part of the broader task of Christian scholarship to help create and sustain a cultural milieu in which the gospel can be heard as an intellectually viable option for thinking men and women. Therefore, the Church has a vital stake in raising up Christian scholars who will help to create a place at the university for Christian ideas. The average Christian does not realize that there is an intellectual war going on in the universities and in the professional journals and scholarly societies. Christianity is being attacked as irrational or obsolete, and millions of students, our future generation of leaders, have absorbed that viewpoint.

This is a war we cannot afford to lose. The great Princeton theologian J. Gresham Machen warned on the eve of the Fundamentalist Controversy that if the church loses the intellectual battle in one generation, then evangelism would become immeasurably more difficult in the next:

> False ideas are the greatest obstacles to the reception of the gospel. We may preach with all the fervor of a reformer and yet succeed only in winning a straggler here and there, if we permit the whole collective thought of the nation or of the world to be controlled by ideas which, by the resistless force of logic, prevent Christianity from being regarded as anything more than a harmless delusion. Under such circumstances, what God desires us to do is to destroy the obstacle at its root.[4]

---

[4] J. Gresham Machen, "Christianity and Culture," *Princeton Theological Review* 11 (1913): 7.

The root of the obstacle is to be found in the university, and it is there that it must be attacked. Unfortunately, Machen's warning went unheeded, and biblical Christianity retreated into the intellectual closets of fundamentalism, from which it has only recently begun to reemerge. The war is not yet lost, and it is one which we must not lose: souls of men and women hang in the balance.

So what are evangelicals doing to win this war? Until recently, very little indeed. Malik asked pointedly,

> Who among evangelicals can stand up to the great secular or naturalistic or atheistic scholars on their own terms of scholarship? Who among evangelical scholars is quoted as a normative source by the greatest secular authorities on history or philosophy or psychology or sociology or politics? Does the evangelical mode of thinking have the slightest chance of becoming the dominant mode in the great universities of Europe and America that stamp our entire civilization with their spirit and ideas?
>
> . . . For the sake of greater effectiveness in witnessing to Jesus Christ Himself, as well as for their own sakes, evangelicals cannot afford to keep on living on the periphery of responsible intellectual existence.[5]

These words hit like a hammer. Evangelicals really have been living on the periphery of responsible intellectual existence. Most prominent evangelical scholars tend to be very big fish in a very small pond. Our influence extends little beyond the evangelical subculture. We tend to publish exclusively with evangelical presses, and therefore our books are likely to go unread by non-evangelical scholars; and instead of participating in the standard professional societies, we are active instead in the evangelical professional societies. As a result, we effectively put our light under a bushel and have little leavening effect for the gospel in our professional fields. In turn, the intellectual drift of the culture at large continues unchecked, deeper into secularism.

---

[5] Malik, "Other Side of Evangelism," 40.

We desperately need Christian scholars who can, as Malik said, compete with non-Christian thinkers in their fields of expertise on their own terms of scholarship. It can be done. There is, for example, a revolution going on right now in the field of philosophy, which, as Malik noted, is the most important domain for thought and intellect, since it is foundational to every other discipline at the university. Christian philosophers have been coming out of the closet and defending the truth of the Christian worldview with philosophically sophisticated arguments in the finest secular journals and professional societies. The face of American philosophy has been changed as a result.

Fifty years ago philosophers widely regarded talk about God as literally meaningless, as mere gibberish, but today no informed philosopher could take such a viewpoint. In fact, many of America's finest philosophers today are outspoken Christians. To give you some feel for the impact of this revolution, I want to quote at some length from an article that appeared in the fall of 2001 in the journal *Philo* lamenting what the author called "the desecularization of academia that evolved in philosophy departments since the late 1960s." The author, himself a prominent atheist philosopher, writes,

> By the second half of the twentieth century, universities . . . had been become [*sic*] in the main secularized. The standard . . . position in each field . . . assumed or involved arguments for a naturalist world-view. . . . Analytic philosophers . . . treated theism as an anti-realist or non-cognitivist world-view, requiring the reality, not of a deity, but merely of emotive expressions or certain "forms of life". . . .
>
> This is not to say that none of the scholars in the various academic fields were realist theists in their "private lives"; but realist theists, for the most part, excluded their theism from their publications and teaching, in large part because theism . . . was mainly considered to have such a low epistemic status that it did not meet the standards of an "academically respectable" position to hold. The secularization of mainstream academia began to quickly unravel upon the publication of Plantinga's influential book, *God and Other*

Minds, in 1967. . . . This book, followed seven years later by Plantinga's even more impressive book, *The Nature of Necessity,* made it manifest that a realist theist was writing at the highest qualitative level of analytic philosophy, on the same playing field as Carnap, Russell, Moore, Grünbaum, and other naturalists. . . .

Naturalists passively watched as realist versions of theism, most influenced by Plantinga's writings, began to sweep through the philosophical community, until today perhaps one-quarter or one-third of philosophy professors are theists, with most being orthodox Christians.

. . . in philosophy, it became, almost overnight, "academically respectable" to argue for theism, making philosophy a favored field of entry for the most intelligent and talented theists entering academia today. . . .

God is not "dead" in academia; he returned to life in the late 1960s and is now alive and well in his last academic stronghold, philosophy departments.[6]

This is the testimony of a prominent atheist philosopher to the change that has taken place before his eyes in American philosophy. I think that he is probably exaggerating when he estimates that one-quarter to one-third of American philosophers are theists, but what his estimates do reveal is the *perceived impact* of Christian philosophers upon this field. Like Gideon's army, a committed minority of activists can have an impact far out of proportion to their numbers. The principal error that he makes is calling philosophy departments God's "last stronghold" at the university. On the contrary, philosophy departments are a *beachhead,* from which operations can be launched to impact other disciplines at the university for Christ.

The point is that the task of desecularization is not hopeless or impossible, nor need significant changes take as long to achieve as one might think. It is this sort of Christian scholarship that represents the best hope for the transformation of culture that Malik and Machen

---

[6] Quentin Smith, "The Metaphilosophy of Naturalism" *Philo* 4/2 (2001).

envisioned, and its true impact for the cause of Christ will only be felt in the next generation, as it filters down into popular culture.

So it can be done! What is sad, however, is how little support the evangelical church gives its thinkers, whom she so desperately needs. It is ironic that it is only after an evangelical student has earned his doctorate that the Christian community pays any attention to him. Once he has his Ph.D., he receives all sorts of invitations to fill speaking engagements, and people ask him to autograph his books for them—but when he was struggling to earn his doctorate he was virtually ignored by the evangelical community or even derided as a "perpetual student." Many of the young men and women who will be needed if the evangelical community is to regain intellectual respectability live on shoestring budgets or go deeply into debt during their years of academic training, alone and forgotten, working under tremendous stress and anxiety and facing an uncertain future.

I consider it a tremendous privilege to set aside a portion of our family's giving to the Lord's work for certain of these young scholars whom we know personally and who will be our Christian leaders of tomorrow. I strongly urge churches to allocate a portion of their yearly budgets for the support of graduate school students from their congregations, especially those attending seminary or completing doctorates. Candidates for such support should be interviewed just like missionary candidates and assessed in terms of their personal spiritual lives, academic abilities, and promise for the future—for the work that they do is just as much a part of the overall evangelistic enterprise as is the work of the missionary. The church cannot in good conscience go on ignoring such people.

What is shocking, too, is how the anti-intellectualism of which Malik spoke has become ensconced even in our evangelical institutions of higher learning. Serious scholarship is often depreciated and impeded, as professors are overburdened with large teaching loads, time-consuming committee assignments, and other administrative chores.

Scholarship seems to be almost last on the list of priorities. My own experience as a full-time seminary professor made clear to me that though there was a strong commitment on the part of the administration to producing pastors, there was very little burden for producing first-rate scholars. Evangelical thought and theology will never assume a leading position in the world so long as this sort of Bible-school mentality reigns.

My personal impressions were confirmed by a sobering report entitled "The State of Scholarship at Evangelical Institutions," a study carried out by University of Notre Dame professor Nathan Hatch and funded by the Pew Charitable Trusts.[7] Hatch discovered that whereas evangelical colleges and seminaries give lip service to scholarship, what they are usually talking about is a broad concept that equates "scholarship" with *any* form of publishing, even on the most popular level. But scholarship narrowly defined as "intensive, time-consuming study and writing on subjects directed at others in one's field" is seriously lacking.

These two concepts of "scholarship" lead to conflicting data: thus the dean of one school reports that 90 percent of the faculty are "actively engaged" in scholarly work, whereas a faculty member *at the same institution* estimates that only 10-15 percent are engaged in scholarship, commenting that the other "75-80 percent *think* they are writing for scholarly audiences. . . . But they don't understand what it is."

Hatch's survey of fifty-eight Christian colleges and seminaries led him to conclude, "For all their dynamism and success in popular communication, evangelicals as a group are failing to sustain a serious intellectual life, conceding intellectual inquiry and discourse to those with secular presuppositions."

This conclusion would be bad enough; but Hatch's survey revealed two more deeply disturbing facts. First, *Christian college and seminary administrators generally do not appreciate serious scholarship and sometimes even impede it.* "The survey shows that college and seminary leadership generally do not make scholarship a priority," writes Hatch. Serious scholarship is "more likely to be seen as superfluous or even opposed to the institution's primary goal," which is either

---

[7] All quotations are from an unpublished copy of the report.

teaching (colleges) or else training pastors (seminaries). With regard to evangelical seminaries, scholarship is valued only "when it contributes to the central goal of training pastors, but not when it takes time away from the classroom." Second, *serious scholarship is seen as irrelevant to one's spiritual life and the life of the church.* Hatch states, "Administrators at evangelical institutions may value scholarship because it enhances teaching or because it enhances the reputation of their schools, but generally scholarship is not regarded as important to the Church's mission or to the spiritual growth of the individual."

He concludes, "Despite the rhetorical emphasis on integration of faith and learning which is commonplace at evangelical institutions, responses to this survey demonstrate that the evangelical academic world as a whole does not connect scholarship with Christian spirituality and the long-term vitality of the Church."

How tragically short-sighted such attitudes are! Machen observed that in his day "many would have the seminaries combat error by attacking it as it is taught by its popular exponents" instead of confusing students "with a lot of German names unknown outside the walls of the university." But to the contrary, Machen insisted, it is essential that Christian scholars be alert to the power of an idea before it has reached popular formulation. Scholarly procedure, he said,

> is based simply upon a profound belief in the pervasiveness of ideas. What is today a matter of academic speculation begins tomorrow to move armies and pull down empires. In that second stage, it has gone too far to be combated; the time to stop it was when it was still a matter of impassionate debate. So as Christians we should try to mold the thought of the world in such a way as to make the acceptance of Christianity something more than a logical absurdity.[8]

Like Malik, Machen also believed that "the chief obstacle to the Christian religion today lies in the sphere of the intellect"[9] and that objections to Christianity must be attacked in that sphere. "The

[8] Machen, "Christianity and Culture," 6.
[9] Ibid., 10.

church is perishing to-day through the lack of thinking, not through an excess of it."[10]

What is ironic about the mentality that says our seminaries should produce pastors, not scholars, is that it is precisely our future pastors, not just our future scholars, who need to be intellectually engaged and to receive this scholarly training. Machen's article was originally given as a speech entitled, "The Scientific Preparation of the Minister." A model for us here ought to be a man like John Wesley, a Spirit-filled revivalist and at the same time an Oxford-educated scholar.

In 1756 Wesley delivered "An Address to the Clergy," which future pastors today ought to read as a part of their training. In discussing what sort of abilities a minister ought to have, Wesley distinguished between "natural gifts" and "acquired abilities." It is extremely instructive to look at the abilities Wesley thought a minister ought to acquire:

(1.) Have I such a knowledge of Scripture, as becomes him who undertakes so to explain it to others, that it may be a light in all their paths? . . . Am I acquainted with the several parts of Scripture; with all parts of the Old Testament and the New? Upon the mention of any text, do I know the context, and the parallel places? . . . Do I know the grammatical construction of the four Gospels; of the Acts; of the Epistles; and am I a master of the spiritual sense (as well as the literal) of what I read? . . . Do I know the objections to them or from them by Jews, Deists, Papists, Socinians, and all other sectaries . . . ? Am I ready to give a satisfactory answer to each of these objections?

(2.) Do I understand Greek and Hebrew? Otherwise, how can I undertake (as every minister does), not only to explain books which are written therein, but to defend them against all opponents? Am I not at the mercy of every one who does understand, or even pretends to understand, the original? . . . Do I understand the language of the New Testament? Am I a critical master of it? . . . If not, how many years did I spend at school? How many at the university? And what was I doing all those years? Ought not shame to cover my face?

---

[10] Ibid., 13.

(3.) Do I understand my own office? Have I deeply considered before God the character which I bear? What is it to be an ambassador of Christ, an envoy from the King of heaven?

(4.) Do I understand so much of profane history as tends to confirm and illustrate the sacred? Am I acquainted with the ancient customs of the Jews and other nations mentioned in Scripture? . . . And am I so far (if no farther) skilled in geography, as to know the situation, and give some account, of all the considerable places mentioned therein?

(5.) Am I a tolerable master of the sciences? Have I gone through the very gate of them, logic? If not, I am not likely to go much farther when I stumble at the threshold. . . . Rather, have not my stupid indolence and laziness made me very ready to believe, what the little wits and pretty gentlemen affirm, "that logic is good for nothing"? It is good for this at least . . . , to make people talk less; by showing them both what is, and what is not, to the point; and how extremely hard it is to prove anything. Do I understand metaphysics; if not the depth of the Schoolmen, the subtleties of Scotus or Aquinas, yet the first rudiments, the general principles, of that useful science? Have I conquered so much of it, as to clear my apprehension and range my ideas under proper heads; so much as enables me to read with ease and pleasure, as well as profit, Dr. Henry Moore's Works, Malebranche's "Search After Truth," and Dr. Clark's "Demonstration of the Being and Attributes of God"? Do I understand natural philosophy? If I have not gone deep therein, have I digested the general ground of it? Have I mastered Gravesande, Keill, Sir Isaac Newton's *Principia,* with his "Theory of Light and Colours"? In order thereto, have I laid in some stock of mathematical knowledge? . . . If I have not gone thus far, if I am such a novice still, what have I been about ever since I came from school?

(6.) Am I acquainted with the Fathers; at least with those venerable men who lived in the earliest ages of the Church? Have I read over and over the golden remains of Clemens Romanus, of Ignatius and Polycarp; and have I given one reading, at least, to the works of Justin Martyr, Tertullian, Origen, Clemens Alexandrinus, and Cyprian?

(7.) Have I any knowledge of the world? Have I studied men (as well as books), and observed their tempers, maxims, and manners? . . . Do I labour never to be rude or ill mannered; . . . am I . . . affable and courteous to all men?

If I am wanting even in these lowest endowments, shall I not frequently regret the want? How often shall I . . . be far less useful than I might have been![11]

Wesley's vision of a pastor is remarkable: a gentleman, skilled in the Scriptures and conversant with history, philosophy, and the science of his day. How do the pastors graduating from our seminaries compare to this model? Church historian and theologian David Wells has called our contemporary generation of pastors "the new disablers" because they have abandoned the traditional role of the pastor as a broker of truth to his congregation and replaced it with a new managerial model drawn from the professional world which emphasizes leadership abilities, marketing, and administration. As a result the Church produces a generation of Christians for whom theology is irrelevant and whose lives outside the church do not differ practically from those of atheists. These new managerial pastors, complains Wells, "are failing the Church and even disabling it. They are leaving it vulnerable to all the seductions of modernity precisely because they have not provided the alternative, which is a view of life centered in God and his truth."[12] We need to recover the traditional model which men like Wesley exemplified.

But finally, it is not just Christian scholars and pastors who need to be intellectually engaged if the Church is to make an impact in our culture. Christian laymen, too, must become intellectually engaged. Our churches are filled with Christians who are idling in intellectual neutral. As Christians, their minds are going to waste. J. P. Moreland in his challenging book *Love Your God with All Your Mind* has called them "empty selves." An empty self is inordinately individualistic, infantile, and narcissistic. It is passive, sensate, busy and hurried, inca-

---

[11] John Wesley, *Works* 6:217-231.
[12] David F. Wells, *No Place for Truth* (Grand Rapids, Mich.: Eerdmans, 1993), 253.

pable of developing an interior life. In what is perhaps the most devastating passage in his book, Moreland asks us to envision a church filled with such people. He asks,

> What would be the theological understanding, . . . the evangelistic courage, the . . . cultural penetration of such a church? . . . If the interior life does not really matter all that much, why spend the time . . . trying to develop an . . . intellectual, spiritually mature life? If someone is basically passive, he or she will just not make the effort to read, preferring instead to be entertained. If a person is sensate in orientation, music, magazines filled with pictures, and visual media in general will be more important than mere words on a page or abstract thoughts. If one is hurried and distracted, one will have little patience for theoretical knowledge and too short . . . an attention span to stay with an idea while it is being carefully developed. . . .
>
> And if someone is overly individualistic, infantile, and narcissistic, what *will* that person read, if he or she reads at all? . . . Christian self-help books that are filled with self-serving content, . . . slogans, simplistic moralizing, a lot of stories and pictures, and inadequate diagnosis of issues that place no demand on the reader. Books about Christian celebrities. . . . what will not be read are books that equip people to . . . develop a well-reasoned, theological understanding of the Christian religion, and fill their role in the broader kingdom of God . . . [Such] a church . . . will become . . . impotent to stand against the powerful forces of secularism that threaten to bury Christian ideas under a veneer of soulless pluralism and misguided scientism. In such a context, the church will be tempted to measure her success largely in terms of numbers—numbers achieved by cultural accommodation to empty selves. In this way, . . . the church will become her own grave digger; her means of short-term "success" will turn out to be the very thing that marginalizes her in the long run.[13]

What makes this description so devastating is that we don't have to imagine such a church; rather this *is* an apt description of far too many American evangelical churches today.

---

[13] J. P. Moreland, *Love Your God with All Your Mind* (Colorado Springs: NavPress, 1997), 93-94.

It is no wonder, then, that despite its resurgence, evangelical Christianity has been so limited in its cultural impact. David Wells reflects,

> The vast growth in evangelically minded people . . . should by now have revolutionized American culture. With a third of American adults now claiming to have experienced spiritual rebirth, a powerful countercurrent of morality growing out of a powerful and alternative worldview should have been unleashed in factories, offices, and board rooms, in the media, universities, and professions, from one end of the country to the other. The results should by now be unmistakable. Secular values should be reeling, and those who are their proponents should be very troubled. But as it turns out, all of this swelling of the evangelical ranks has passed unnoticed in the culture. . . . The presence of evangelicals in American culture has barely caused a ripple.[14]

Sometimes people would justify their lack of intellectual engagement by asserting that they prefer having a "simple faith." But here I think we must distinguish between a childlike faith and a childish faith. A childlike faith is a whole-souled trust in God as one's loving Heavenly Father, and Jesus commends such a faith to us. But a childish faith is an immature, unreflective faith, and such a faith is not commended to us. On the contrary, Paul says, "Do not be children in your thinking; be babes in evil, but in thinking be mature" (1 Cor. 14:20, RSV). If a "simple" faith means an unreflective, ignorant faith, then we should want none of it. In my own life, I can testify that, after many years of study, my worship of God is deeper precisely because of, and not in spite of, my philosophical and theological studies. In every area I have intensely researched—creation, the resurrection, divine omniscience, divine eternity—my appreciation of God's truth and my awe of His person have become more profound. I am excited about future study because of the deeper appreciation I am sure it will bring me of God's person and work. Christian faith is not an apathetic

---

[14] Wells, *No Place for Truth*, 293.

faith, a brain-dead faith, but a living, inquiring faith. As Anselm put it, ours is a faith that seeks understanding.

Furthermore, the results of being in intellectual neutral extend far beyond one's own self. If Christian laymen do not become intellectually engaged, then we are in serious danger of losing our youth. In high school and college, Christian teenagers are intellectually assaulted by every manner of non-Christian philosophy conjoined with an overwhelming relativism. As I speak in churches around the country, I constantly meet parents whose children have lost their faith because there was no one in the church to answer their questions.

Some years ago I had the privilege of getting to know Dr. Blanchard Demerchant, now a philosophy professor. Raised in a Christian home, Blanchard began as a teenager to ask questions concerning doubts about the Christian faith that were troubling him. He went away to Bible college, but to his dismay, found that none of the teachers could address his questions. Yet there was in the administration one well-educated man. Blanchard made an appointment with him, hoping to find some answers to his questions. But when Blanchard had laid out his questions, the administrator, instead of dealing with them, merely commanded Blanchard to get down on his knees and repent before God for entertaining such doubts.

Needless to say, that travesty only convinced Blanchard even more that there was nothing intellectually to the Christian faith. He began to study philosophy at a secular university, became an atheist, convinced the Christian girl whom he had married to likewise abandon her faith, was drafted and sent to Vietnam, where he became a drug addict and alcoholic, and later returned to find his marriage, his job, and his world generally falling apart. He nearly committed suicide. But instead, he began to study and ponder the teaching of the man Jesus, and slowly, painfully, he began to return to the Christian faith. To make a long story short, he is now a transformed person, is reunited with his wife, Phyllis, and has a remarkable ministry with secular university students in philosophy by subtly introducing Christian perspective on philosophical problems in the classroom.

He told me with a smile that his students are simply dumbfounded that he can be both a philosopher and a Christian. Blanchard's story had a happy ending. But for many other children from Christian families the outcome is more tragic.

There can be no question that the church has dropped the ball in this area. But the structures are in place in the church for remedying this problem, if only we will make use of them. I am speaking, of course, of adult Sunday school programs. Why not begin to utilize Sunday school classes to offer laymen serious instruction in such subjects as Christian doctrine, church history, New Testament Greek, apologetics, and so forth? Think of the potential for change! Why not?

I believe that our culture can be changed. I am excited about the renaissance in Christian philosophy in my generation, which bodes well for the next. Whether God is calling you to become a Christian scholar on the front lines of intellectual battle, a Christian pastor to serve as a broker of truth to your congregation, or a Christian layman or parent who is always ready to give a reason for the hope that is in you, we have the awesome opportunity of being agents of cultural change in Christ's name.[15] For the church's sake, for your own sakes, for your future children's sake, do not squander this opportunity! So if, up until now, you've just been coasting, idling in intellectual neutral, now is the time to get it in gear! In the following chapters, we shall, with minds fully engaged, explore some of the difficult questions confronting Christians in contemporary Western culture.

Answers to the Quiz

1. Church father (354–430) and the author of *The City of God* who emphasized God's unmerited grace.
2. The church council that in 325 officially ratified the doctrine of the equal deity of the Father and the Son as opposed to the view held by the Arian heretics.
3. The doctrine that in God there are three persons in one being.

---

[15] Having heard the call, we face the next step of equipping ourselves for battle. By reading this book, you have already begun. A good second step is to read Moreland's *Love Your God with All Your Mind* and pursue the relevant references in his bibliographies sorted by field of specialization.

4. The doctrine enunciated at the Council of Chalcedon (451) affirming the true deity and true humanity of Christ.

5. The view that the world and God are identical.

6. A medieval Catholic theologian (1225–1274) and the author of *Summa Theologiae,* whose views have been determinative for traditional Roman Catholic theology.

7. The origin of Protestantism in the sixteenth century in the efforts of men such as Luther, Calvin, and Zwingli to reform the doctrine and practice of the Roman Catholic church; it emphasized justification by grace through faith alone and the exclusive authority of the Bible.

8. The Roman Catholic monk (1483–1546) who started the Protestant Reformation and was the founder of Lutheranism.

9. The doctrine that by His death on our behalf and in our place Christ reconciled us to God.

10. The intellectual revolt in Europe during the seventeenth and eighteenth centuries against the authority of church and monarchy in the name of human autonomy; also called the Age of Reason.

1

DOUBT

Any Christian who is intellectually engaged and reflecting about his faith will inevitably face the problem of doubt. This problem, I believe, must be very seriously addressed. Too often Christian leaders give lip service to the importance of the mind and the quest after truth, but have a sort of glib confidence that such a quest will invariably wind up at the truth of Christianity. But such a result is by no means guaranteed. During the 1960s, for example, when I was an undergraduate, many brilliant students passed through the doors of Wheaton College (Illinois), but those years were also characterized by widespread doubt, cynicism, and unbelief with regard to the faith. I came to Wheaton at the tail end of the sixties, and it troubled me deeply to see some of my classmates, whose intellectual abilities I admired, lose their faith and, to all appearances, reject Christ. This brought home to me in a powerful way how serious the problem of doubt can be.

And yet the church tends to shuffle this problem under the rug. How many sermons have you ever heard on how to deal with doubt in your Christian life? I know of only a couple of books on this subject. Perhaps because Christians aren't supposed to have any doubts, we smile and pretend that this problem doesn't exist. But it does, and nobody is exempt.

Some years ago, for example, while I was on sabbatical at the University of Arizona in Tucson, the pastor of the Baptist church my

wife and I were attending stood up and announced to his congregation that he had experienced a great spiritual victory, which he wanted
to share: for the past year he had doubted whether God exists, but
now those doubts had been resolved and he felt a new confidence in
the Lord! I was so surprised by this admission—who would have
thought that this successful pastor of a burgeoning church had
doubted that there even is a God? I greatly respected him for his hon-
esty, for what his testimony communicated to his people was that they
should not be ashamed of their doubts, when they had them, but
could admit them and work through them and seek the help of their
pastor, who had walked down that lonely road himself.

A Christian who is thinking for himself will confront doubts; and
doubt, if not properly dealt with, can be tremendously destructive of
one's spiritual life. You may confront objections to, or intellectual difficulties with, the Christian faith that you cannot answer, and these
unanswered questions may lead you to doubt that Christianity is true.
Those doubts then begin to gnaw away at the vitality of your spiritual
experience: *Maybe it's all an illusion,* you think. *Maybe I'm just kidding
myself.* Your devotional life begins to lag or grow dry, for how can you
devote yourself to someone who maybe isn't there? Why go on
deceiving yourself? That feeling then deadens you to speaking of
Christ to others. As one seminary student who was struggling with
doubt told me, "How could I tell someone else to receive Christ
when I wasn't even sure myself that it was the truth?"

Pretty soon you're on a downward spiral that you can't seem to
stop. But externally you continue to put on a good face and go to
church. You can't admit your doubts to others—what would they
think? And so a sort of secret battle rages within, destroying your spiritual life from the inside out, leaving you an empty shell. To make
matters worse, you sense your own hypocrisy, and this only serves to
add the burden of guilt to the load of doubt you already bear. What
can be done? Is there any antidote to doubt?

Well, to begin with, we have to admit that there are no easy
answers to the problem of doubt. There is no simple, quick recipe
that if followed will make your doubts vanish like magic. You will

probably have to work through your doubts in a slow and agonizing process. You may have to endure what saints have called "the dark night of the soul," or "the dark valley," before coming into the light again; but be assured that many, many great men and women of God have traveled that same path before you and have emerged victorious at the end. Your struggle is not unique, and there is hope of a happy ending.

But what can you do to speed your journey along that path, or better, to avoid it? Let me make four practical suggestions.

First, recognize that doubt is never a purely intellectual problem. There is a spiritual dimension to the problem that must be recognized. Never lose sight of the fact that you are involved in a spiritual warfare and that there is an enemy of your soul who hates you intensely, whose goal is your destruction, and who will stop at nothing to destroy you. Paul reminds us that "our struggle is not against flesh and blood, but against the rulers, against the authorities, against the powers of this dark world and against the spiritual forces of evil in the heavenly realms" (Eph. 6:12). Doubt is not just a matter of academic debate or disinterested intellectual discussion; it involves a battle for your very soul, and if Satan can use doubt to immobilize you or destroy you, then he will.

Unfortunately, the spiritual dimension inherent in the problem of doubt is often ignored by those involved in higher learning. When I was an undergraduate at Wheaton College, an attitude was prevalent among the students that doubt was actually a virtue and that a Christian who did not doubt his faith was somehow intellectually deficient or naive. But such an attitude is unbiblical and confused. It is unbiblical to think of doubt as a virtue; to the contrary, doubt is always portrayed in the Scriptures as something detrimental to spiritual life. Doubt never builds up; it always destroys. How could the students I knew at Wheaton College have got things so totally reversed? It is probably because they had confused *thinking* about their faith with *doubting* their faith. Thinking about your faith is, indeed, a virtue, for it helps you to better understand and defend your faith. But thinking about your faith is not equivalent to doubting your faith.

We need to keep the distinction clear. A student came up to me once after one of my lectures and said, "How come everything you say confirms what my pastor has always taught?" Somewhat amazed, I laughed and said, "Why shouldn't it?" He replied, "Well, all of the other men in the department challenge my faith." My response was, "Look, I don't want to challenge your *faith;* I want to challenge your *thinking.* But I want to *build up* your faith."

My experience as a young Christian of seeing some of my college classmates lose their faith left a deep impression on me, and when I began teaching I resolved to do all I could to help my students stay in the faith while still exploring the intellectual issues about the faith. In particular, I resolved never to present objections to Christianity without also presenting and defending various solutions to those objections. One of my colleagues who did not follow this method was causing some concern among certain Christian students in his classes. "I was only trying to get them to think," he explained to me. "I was just playing the devil's advocate."

Those words hit me like a dash of cold water. For him they were merely a manner of speaking, but it was their literal sense that struck me. *Playing the devil's advocate.* Think of it: to be Satan's advocate in the classroom! That is something we must never allow ourselves to become. As Christian teachers, students, and laymen, we must never lose sight of the wider spiritual battle in which we are all involved and so must be extremely wary of what we say or write, lest we become the instruments of Satan in destroying someone else's faith. We can challenge people to think more deeply and rigorously about their Christian faith without encouraging them to doubt their faith.

Of course, in thinking about your faith, you are going to confront difficulties or objections that may cause doubt. But the first point I am trying to emphasize is that when that happens, don't be deceived into thinking that this is merely an intellectual struggle; there is a deeper spiritual dimension to it as well. "Be self-controlled and alert," Peter warns, for "your enemy the devil prowls around like a roaring lion looking for someone to devour" (1 Pet. 5:8). Don't be so naive as to think that the devil isn't involved in the intellectual arena, too. We must be ever vigilant, as Paul says, "in order that Satan might not outwit us. For we are not unaware of his schemes" (2 Cor. 2:11). In particular, Paul warns us not to let anyone make a prey of us "through hollow and deceptive philosophy, which depends on human tradition and the basic principles of this world rather than on Christ" (Col. 2:8).

When doubts come, then, don't try to hide them or pretend they don't exist. Take them to God in prayer and ask Him to help you resolve them. Tell Him honestly that, say, you doubt His existence, or His being in Christ, or whatever doubt you may have. He cares for you and will help you. I love the prayer of the man who came to Jesus and cried, "I do believe; help me overcome my unbelief!" (Mark 9:24). And what a comfort it is to know that Jesus accepted such a prayer and such faith and responded positively to it! When we have intellectual doubts, that is the time as never before to deepen our spiritual lives and seek the fullness of God's Spirit.

Second, when doubts arise, keep in mind the proper relationship between faith and reason. The question here is, How do I know that my faith is true? Do I know it on the basis of reason and evidence? Or do I know its truth by faith itself? Or is my faith founded on authority, or perhaps on mystical experience? How do I know that my Christian faith is true?

As I read the New Testament, the answer is that we know our faith is true by the self-authenticating witness of the Holy Spirit within us. What do I mean by that? I mean that we do not *infer* that our faith is true based on any sort of evidence or proof, but that in the context of the Spirit of God's speaking to our hearts, we see immediately and unmistakably that our faith is true. God's Spirit makes it evident to us that our faith is true.

Look briefly with me at what the apostles Paul and John had to say about this matter. According to Paul, every Christian is indwelt with the Holy Spirit, and it is the witness of the Spirit that gives us assurance of being God's children: "For you did not receive a spirit that makes you a slave again to fear, but you received the Spirit of sonship. And by him we cry, '*Abba,* Father.' The Spirit himself testifies with our spirit that we are God's children" (Rom. 8:15-16). Elsewhere, Paul speaks of this assurance as "the full riches of complete understanding" (Col. 2:2) and as "deep conviction" (1 Thess. 1:5). Sometimes we call this experience "assurance of salvation." Now, clearly, salvation entails that God exists, that Christ atoned for our sins, that He rose from the dead, and so forth, so that if you are assured of your salvation, then you must be assured of all these other truths as well. Hence, the witness of the Holy Spirit gives the believer an immediate assurance that his faith is true.

The apostle John teaches the same thing and explicitly contrasts this assurance with an assurance based on evidence and argument. He begins with a reminder to his Christian readers: "But you have an anointing from the Holy One, and all of you know the truth. . . . As for you, the anointing you received from him remains in you, and you do not need anyone to teach you. But as his anointing teaches you about all things and as that anointing is real, not counterfeit—just as it has taught you, remain in him" (1 John 2:20, 27). Here the anointing of the Holy Spirit, which every Christian enjoys, is the source of our knowing the truth about our faith. John then goes on to contrast the confidence the Spirit of God brings with the assurance brought by human evidence: "For there are three that testify: the Spirit, the water and the blood; and the three are in agreement. We accept man's testimony, but God's testimony is greater because it is the testimony of God, which he has given about his Son. Anyone who believes in the Son of God has this testimony in his heart" (1 John 5:7-10a). The "water" here probably refers to Jesus' baptism, and the "blood" to His crucifixion, those two events being the ones that marked the beginning and the end of His earthly ministry. "Man's testimony" is the apostolic witness to the ministry of Jesus from His baptism to His crucifixion. Yet John declares that even though we quite rightly receive this testimony, still the inner testimony of the Holy Spirit is greater. Such a statement is remarkable because in his Gospel John had laid great weight precisely on the apostolic testimony: "these [signs] are written that you may believe that Jesus is the Christ, the Son of God. . . . This is the disciple who testifies to these things

and who wrote them down. We know that his testimony is true"
(John 20:31; 21:24). But here in his first epistle he asserts that the
knowledge inspired by the Holy Spirit is even more certain than
the testimony of the apostles themselves.

The view of the New Testament, then, is that fundamentally we
know our faith to be true by the self-authenticating witness of God's
Holy Spirit.[1]

What role, then, is left for reason to play? Here I think a distinction made by the Protestant Reformer Martin Luther can be of help.
Luther distinguished between what he called the *magisterial* and the
ministerial uses of reason. In the magisterial use of reason, reason sits
over and above the gospel like a magistrate and judges whether it is
true or false. In the ministerial use of reason, reason submits to and
serves the gospel as a handmaiden. Luther maintained that only the
ministerial use of reason is legitimate, and from what I have just said,
we can see that he was right. It is a usurpation of the role properly
belonging to the Holy Spirit Himself for reason to assume the magisterial role. For it is the Holy Spirit who teaches us directly the truth
of the gospel, and reason has no right to contradict Him.

Instead, reason's role is that of a servant. Reason is a God-given
instrument to help us better understand and defend our faith.
Though the Holy Spirit gives us assurance of the basic truth of our
faith, He does not impart knowledge of all its ramifications and ins
and outs—for example, whether God is timeless or everlasting, how
to reconcile providence and free will, or how to formulate the doctrine of the Trinity. Those are things we must decide by thinking
about them.

As Anselm put it, ours is a faith that seeks understanding. In a similar way, reason can be used to defend our faith by formulating arguments for the existence of God or by refuting objections. But though
the arguments so developed serve to confirm the truth of our faith,

---

[1] Readers who wish to pursue further such an approach to a religious theory of knowledge may prof-
itably consult Alvin Plantinga, *Warranted Christian Belief* (Oxford: Oxford University Press, 2001).
My main difference from Plantinga is that whereas he conceives of the witness of the Holy Spirit
as akin to an (external) cognitive faculty, I think it is more accurately taken to be part of the circumstances that ground Christian belief.

they are not properly the basis of our faith, for that is supplied by the witness of the Holy Spirit Himself. Even if there were no arguments in defense of the faith, our faith would still have its firm foundation.

Now what is the implication of all this for the problem of doubt? Simply this: *doubt is controllable so long as reason does not usurp the magisterial role.* So long as reason operates in its ministerial role, the spiritual assurance of our faith cannot be undermined. It is only when we allow reason to usurp the magisterial role and take the place of the Holy Spirit that doubt becomes dangerous.

This is not to say that Christianity cannot stand up to reason. On the contrary, I believe that someone who had all the facts and never made a mistake would, if he followed the magisterial role of reason, conclude that Christianity is true. Of course, such a person would also be God and therefore hardly need any proof! But the point is that people in different times and places and with differing abilities and opportunities do not have all the facts and do make errors in reasoning. In certain historical circumstances, the evidence available may be against Christianity. If persons in those situations repressed and ignored the witness of the Holy Spirit and followed instead the magisterial role of reason, they would be led to unbelief.

On the other hand, if we attend to the witness of the Spirit and do not allow reason to transgress its proper function, then we shall not lose faith even when we are confronted with objections that we, with our limited abilities, cannot refute. Alvin Plantinga, a great Christian philosopher, provides a helpful illustration of what I mean. He invites us to imagine the following scenario:

> I am applying to the National Endowment for the Humanities for a fellowship, I write a letter to a colleague, trying to bribe him to write the Endowment a glowing letter on my behalf; he indignantly refuses and sends the letter to my chairman. The letter disappears from the chairman's office under mysterious circumstances. I have a motive for stealing it; I have the opportunity to do so; and I have been known to do such things in the past. Furthermore, an extremely reliable member of the department claims to have seen

me furtively entering the chairman's office at about the time when the letter must have been stolen. The evidence against me is very strong; my colleagues reproach me for such underhanded behavior and treat me with evident distaste. The facts of the matter, however, are that I didn't steal the letter and in fact spent the entire afternoon in question on a solitary walk in the woods; furthermore, I clearly remember spending that afternoon walking in the woods.

In such a case, all the evidence stands against me and yet I know I am not guilty. For the evidence cannot overcome the more basic knowledge I have of the truth of my innocence. Even if the evidence is irrefutable, such that others ought to think me guilty, I myself am not obliged to go along with the evidence, for I know better.[2]

In the same way, given the witness of the Spirit in my life, giving me an immediate assurance of the truth of my faith, I needn't be shaken when objections come along that I can't answer. For I have a foundation for my faith that is deeper and more sure than the shifting sands of evidence and argument.

The point is this: the secret to dealing with doubt in the Christian life is not to resolve all of one's doubts, for that is probably impossible in a finite lifetime. One will always have unanswered questions. Rather, the secret is learning to live victoriously with one's unanswered questions. By understanding the true foundation of our faith and by assigning to reason its proper role, we can prevent unanswered questions from turning into destructive doubts. In such a case, we shall not have answers to all our questions, but in a deeper sense that will not matter. For we shall know that our faith is true on the basis of the Spirit's witness, and we can live confidently even while having questions we cannot answer. That is why it is so important to keep in mind the proper relationship between faith and reason.

Third, remember the frailty of our limited intellects and knowledge. Socrates said that he was the wisest man in Athens because he knew that he knew nothing. The apostle Paul, when confronted with Greek Gnostics, who touted the importance of knowledge, took a similar

---

[2] Alvin Plantinga, "The Foundations of Theism: A Reply," *Faith and Philosophy* 3 (1986): 310.

line. "Knowledge," he wrote, "puffs up, but love builds up. The man who thinks he knows something does not yet know as he ought to know. But the man who loves God is known by God" (1 Cor. 8:1b-3). According to Paul, if you think you're so smart that you've got it all figured out about God, then in fact you don't know anything. You're just an inflated intellectual blowhard. By contrast, the person who loves God is the one who truly has come to know Him.

Such a doctrine has shattering implications for our proud intellectual attainments. It means that the simplest child of God who lives in love is wiser in God's sight than the most brilliant Bertrand Russell the world has ever seen.

We as Christians need to realize the feebleness and finitude of our human knowledge. I can honestly testify that the more I learn, the more desperately ignorant I feel. Further study only serves to open up to one's consciousness all the endless vistas of knowledge, even in one's own field, about which one knows absolutely nothing. I can identify with a statement Isaac Newton once made, reflecting back on his discoveries laid out in his great treatise on physics, the *Principia mathematica*. He said,

> I do not know what I may appear to the world, but to myself I seem to have been only like a boy playing on the sea-shore, and diverting myself in now and then finding a smoother pebble or a prettier shell than ordinary, whilst the great ocean of truth lay all undiscovered before me.[3]

When my wife and I were living in England during my Ph.D. work, I visited the great historian of philosophy Frederick C. Copleston in London. He had spent his entire life writing a massive, nine-volume *History of Philosophy* from the ancient Greeks through the twentieth century, as well as numerous works on such subjects as Oriental philosophy and Russian philosophy. I asked him if, after this lifetime of study, he had learned some overriding lesson from the history of philosophy. He replied that he had, and then explained that

---

[3] Quoted in *Brewster's Memoirs of Newton,* vol. 2, chapter 27.

when he started the project he had hoped to show how the philosophy of Thomas Aquinas was the age-lasting philosophy. But it soon became evident to him that it was impossible to do that. Instead, what his study of the history of thought had shown him, he said, was how bound any man's philosophy is to the day and age in which he lives, to the thought-forms of his era and culture, to the intellectual milieu in which he writes. That did not mean that Copleston was a relativist; it meant that we have to be very cautious in our claims to have discovered some truth and very modest about our own intellectual attainments.

What application does Copleston's point have to the problem of doubt? It means that we should be cautious, indeed, about thinking that we have come upon the decisive disproof of our faith. It is pretty unlikely that we have found the irrefutable objection. The history of philosophy is littered with the wrecks of such objections. Given the confidence that the Holy Spirit inspires, we should esteem lightly the arguments and objections that generate our doubts.

I shudder when I read the words of certain non-Christian philosophers who solemnly claim to have proved, say, that God cannot be omnipotent, or that God cannot be omniscient, or that miracles are impossible, or some such dogmatic assertion. Some time ago I read an article by a philosopher who claimed to have proved that God cannot know that He is God! The problem with such an article is not just that its conclusion is based on a ludicrously fallacious argument. The point is rather that the article is in a real sense blasphemous. It represents philosophy at its worst, the sort Paul warned against in Colossians 2:8. If with our limited intellects and resources we cannot discover the resolution to some objection or to an apparent antinomy, such as that between divine foreknowledge and human freedom, rather than doubt or deny the Christian faith at that point, we ought simply to hold the truth in tension and admit that the difficulty lies in our own lack of insight into the problem and its solution. We need to remember the frailty of our limited intellects and knowledge.

Fourth, pursue your doubts into the ground. We've seen that the secret to handling doubt in our lives is not to resolve every question but *to learn to live victoriously with unresolved questions.* Any thinking Christian will have a "question bag" filled with unresolved difficulties he must learn to live with. But from time to time, as you have opportunity, it's good to take the bag down from the shelf, select one of the questions, and go to work on answering it. Indeed, I can say that working hard on an unresolved question and pursuing it until you finally find an answer that satisfies you intellectually is one of the most exhilarating experiences of the Christian life. To resolve a doubt that has troubled you for some time brings a wonderful sense of intellectual peace and inspires confidence that there are solutions to the remaining difficulties in your question bag.

When you have a doubt or a question about a particular issue, set aside time to study that issue by reading books or articles on the subject. Libraries at Christian colleges and seminaries can be particularly helpful, if those are available where you live. Even public libraries can order what you need through their interlibrary loan service. Find out what Christian scholars have written in the area you are exploring and write to them—or, if possible, visit them to discuss your question. Seek out and talk with those members of the Body of Christ who have studied the subject. In that way, the members of the Body will be helping to build each other up. But don't let your doubts just sit there: pursue them and keep after them until you drive them into the ground.

Doubt can be an agonizing experience in the Christian life, and there is no "quick fix" for resolving it. It requires patience and endurance. But I believe you will find the four points I've mentioned helpful in handling doubt. May God give us by the Holy Spirit the gift of faith that we may triumph over doubt and take every thought captive to obey Christ!

2

UNANSWERED PRAYER

Whatever you ask in My name, I will do it," Jesus promised. In fact, Jesus repeats this promise three times in different words in John 14, 15, and 16. "And I will do whatever you ask in my name" (John 14:13a); "Then the Father will give you whatever you ask in my name" (15:16b); "My Father will give you whatever you ask in my name" (16:23b). Jesus evidently really meant business. That is a wonderful, astounding claim.

But the problem is that this promise just does not seem to be unqualifiedly true. Often preachers may exhort us to lay hold of the promise in our personal lives, to believe it, and claim it for ourselves. But the problem is that we can't believe the promise because it is simply unbelievable in its unqualified form. For if we are ruthlessly honest with ourselves, every one of us knows that sometimes God does not answer our prayers.

Indeed, sometimes He *cannot* answer our prayers because Christians are praying for contradictory things. When I was a student at Wheaton, I heard about two guys who were both in love with the same girl. Each one was praying that God would turn her affections toward him so that he might marry her. Now clearly the prayers of at least one of those young men was going to be unanswered. God couldn't answer them both because their prayers were contradictory.

Or imagine two Christian athletes playing on opposite sides in the Super Bowl or in the World Series. Each would naturally be disposed to pray that his team would win, and yet both prayers could not be answered, for the two athletes would be praying for contradictory results.

But on an even more everyday level, every one of us has experienced unanswered prayer. We have asked God to do something, something we think will glorify Him, and we have prayed in faith believing—and God didn't come through. Sometimes unanswered prayer of this kind involves cases of prayer for healing. One church I knew of prayed for the miraculous healing of one of its members. The people really believed God and were expecting a miracle. But the man died. Many people were deeply shaken in their Christian faith; they had asked God in faith for something in Jesus' name and He did not do it. Perhaps Jesus' promise was not true after all—maybe the Christian faith was not true after all.

And it's not just Christian laymen who confront this problem. Christian spiritual leaders also experience unanswered prayer. I once heard Cliff Barrows say that his partners on the Billy Graham team had long ago ceased to pray for good weather for their crusades— indeed, some of their best crusades had been held in the rain. In his seminars Bill Gothard tells one incredible story after another about how God brought in the money to pay the bills, but he also admits, "In all fairness to God, He did not always come through in the nick of time." In other words, some prayers went unanswered.

Now someone might say, "But you can't use human experience to qualify God's promises!" But the problem with this response is that the Scriptures themselves give examples of unanswered prayer. Think of Paul's so-called "thorn in the flesh"—a physical ailment he asked God three times to remove (2 Cor. 12:7). But God did not remove it. Paul also asked the Roman church to pray that he might be delivered from the unbelievers in Jerusalem on what turned out to be his final visit there (Rom. 15:31). But he was not delivered; instead we read in Acts 21 of Paul's arrest in Jerusalem and the imprisonment that eventually led to his martyrdom. So even the Scriptures themselves give examples of unanswered prayer. It is not unqualifiedly true that whatever we ask in Jesus' name we shall receive.

But this is very troubling. For Jesus promised that whatever we asked in His name we would receive. So is His promise empty? Worse still, how can Jesus be God if He makes empty promises? How does one solve the problem of unanswered prayer?

First, let's look at inadequate solutions to this problem that are often used by Christians today. One solution is simply to deny that prayer ever goes unanswered. This is the most radical solution, and yet it is sometimes espoused by well-meaning Christians. For example, when my wife, Jan, and I were on Campus Crusade staff at Northern Illinois University, our movement was infiltrated by certain Christians who believed that physical healing was included in the atonement of Christ, and thus no Christian ever needed to be sick. Just pray to God and He will heal you!

Well, the result of this was that some of our students were throwing away their glasses, claiming that they were healed, even though they couldn't see any better. I remember confronting one of them by asking, "Are you healed?" He said, "Yes, I am." So I said, "Well, can you see any better?" "No," he admitted. "So then how are you healed if you can't see any better?" I asked. "Because my faith isn't strong enough," he said. "I am healed, but I just don't have faith to believe it." And so these poor, nearsighted students were going around trying to study and attend classes without their glasses, claiming that they were healed but that they lacked the faith to believe that God had answered their prayers. I wonder what those Christians would say about someone who died from cancer despite prayers for healing: that he really was alive and well but just appeared to be dead because he lacked the faith? What those Christians needed was not more faith but some common sense!

A less radical but nevertheless inadequate solution often proposed is that God always answers prayer but that His answers may vary between yes, no, and wait. Thus, a prayer that receives a negative answer is not really an unanswered prayer. God did answer, namely, by saying no. But this solution is just playing at words. What we mean by unanswered prayer is prayer that receives a negative answer. Jesus promised that whatever we ask in His name we shall receive. It does nothing to solve the problem for someone to say that God *did* answer your prayer but said no, for the promise is that he will always say yes. So the problem remains the same, just under different words, namely, How can there be negatively answered prayer?

A third inadequate solution that Christians sometimes use is to rationalize things away so that they can say God answered prayer after all. Once I was at a meeting where prayer was offered for God to help a seriously ill man get out of the hospital. But the following day the man died. At our next meeting the speaker who had led in prayer the night before announced the man's death and proclaimed triumphantly that our prayers had been answered. "We asked God to take him out of the hospital, and, praise the Lord, He has!" Well, this sort of rationalization strikes me as basically dishonest. It was clear that the intent of our prayers the night before was that God would heal the man. Rationalizing away a negative answer to prayer is to view God as a great genie from Aladdin's lamp who fulfills the technical language of our requests but misses the intent altogether, so that we wind up with something totally different from what we requested. That is not the God of the Bible. Why not be honest and admit that God just did not answer the prayer?

So I think the proper solution lies in a different direction. I do not think that Jesus' promise is empty, but I do think that it must be qualified. It is not true simply and without qualification that you will receive whatever you ask in Jesus' name. The promise must be qualified in certain ways in accordance with the teaching of the rest of Scripture.

Now qualifying the promise may sound distressing to you, but let me point out that there are precedents for doing so. Other teachings of Jesus also have to be qualified in light of different Scriptures. Take Jesus' teachings on divorce, for example. In Mark 10:11, Jesus makes the blanket statement, "Anyone who divorces his wife and marries another woman commits adultery against her." No exception is allowed. But in Matthew 19:9 Jesus says, "I tell you that anyone who divorces his wife, except for marital unfaithfulness, and marries another woman commits adultery." Here the former statement is qualified: there is an exception which permits divorce after all, namely, marital unfaithfulness on the part of a spouse. Now I'm suggesting that Jesus' promises about prayer also need to be qualified in this way. Implicit in Jesus' blanket promise are certain important qualifiers, and if those qualifiers are not met, one cannot claim the promise.

What are some of these implicit qualifications to Jesus' promise? Many of them can be classed under the heading "Obstacles to Answered Prayer." Let's look at some of them.

1. *Sin in our lives.* The most basic and, I think, prevalent obstacle to answered prayer is unconfessed sin in our lives. Jesus' promise naturally presupposes that the person praying is a Christian living in the fullness and power of the Holy Spirit. A Christian who is living in unconfessed sin or in the power of the flesh can have no confidence that his prayers will be answered. The psalmist said, "If I had cherished sin in my heart, the Lord would not have listened" (Ps. 66:18). In what must be a terribly convicting verse to us married men, Peter writes that husbands should live considerately with their wives, bestowing honor on the physically weaker sex, in order that their prayers may not be hindered (see 1 Pet. 3:7). Think of it: not treating your wife right hinders your prayers! Jesus' promise assumes that the believer is abiding in Christ, keeping His commandments, walking in the light, filled with the Spirit, and loving the brethren. When you think about this, it's only by God's grace that any of our prayers are answered!

2. *Wrong motives.* Many times our prayers go unanswered because our motives are wrong. Too often, our prayers are motivated by selfishness—a sort of "Gimme, gimme, gimme" attitude centered wholly on ourselves. Jesus had promised, "Ask and it will be given to you" (Matt. 7:7), but James explained to his readers, "When you ask, you do not receive, because you ask with wrong motives, that you may spend what you get on your pleasures" (James 4:3). Prayer that is totally self-centered does not fall under Jesus' promise.

48　HARD QUESTIONS, REAL ANSWERS

I remember once reading a tract on why there is no revival in the church today. One of the reasons was depicted in a cartoon labeled "A Modern Saint Struggles with the Forces of Darkness." It was a picture of a man kneeling by his bedside contending with God in prayer: "Oh Lord, please give us that new color television set! You know how much we need it. Please, Lord, please, help us get that color TV!" The correct motive for our prayer requests should be God's glory. Hence, in the Old Testament one often finds prayers based on the desire that God would do some act for the sake of His name. It was Jesus' prayer that God would glorify His name (see John 12:28). This should be our motive in prayer: to request things of God, not that our selfish desires might be satisfied, but that His name might be glorified.

3. *Lack of faith.* Jesus Himself made clear that only believing prayer can be assured of an answer. He told the disciples, "Whatever you ask for in prayer, believe that you have received it, and it will be yours" (Mark 11:24). Here the promise is qualified such that prayer must be accompanied by faith. If you have faith that God will answer your request and you do not doubt, then He will answer it. By contrast, the man who is ridden by doubts cannot have any confidence that his prayer will be answered. Thus, James says, speaking of someone's prayer for wisdom, "When he asks, he must believe and not doubt, because he who doubts is like a wave of the sea, blown and tossed by the wind. That man should not think he will receive anything from the Lord; he is a double-minded man, unstable in all he does" (James 1:6-8).

Of course, this statement raises all sorts of difficult questions about how one acquires that kind of faith and how such a faith can be sustained in the face of unanswered prayer. I'm not going to try to treat such questions now. Let me just note that Jesus also said that the faith required need not be great, but that mighty things can happen as a result of faith as small as a grain of mustard seed (see Luke 17:6); and let us also remember that faith is a gift of God. We can always pray, "Lord, I believe! Help thou mine unbelief" (Mark 9:24, KJV). In any case, my main point here is that one more qualification must be introduced into Jesus' promise: we must pray in faith.

4. *Lack of earnestness.* Sometimes our prayers are not answered because, quite frankly, we don't really care whether they are. We casually pray in the prayer meeting for some request and then forget all about it. We hardly ever think to ask later how that prayer was answered. We don't really care. That's why, when Jan and I were involved in raising financial support for our ministry in Europe, we were pretty unimpressed when someone said, "I'll pray for you." Usually what that really meant was, "I'm not interested enough to support you financially." But if that's true, then I honestly doubt that he's interested enough to pray earnestly, either.

Unfortunately, Christians have the idea that prayer support is a lesser commitment than financial support, when in reality precisely the opposite is the case. It doesn't take much effort to write a check every month or so and never think of it again, but it's tough to pray earnestly and regularly for a missionary or Christian worker. It is precisely this earnest prayer, however, this serious, heartfelt, get-down-to-business-with-God prayer, that God attends to. Read the great prayers of the Bible and ask yourself if those people were earnest or not. A beautiful example is Hannah's prayer for a son in 1 Samuel 1. She was so intense in her prayer, so oblivious to everything going on around her, that the priest at the house of the Lord thought she was drunk! But of course the supreme example was Jesus Himself, a man who would continue all night in prayer to God, who literally wore the disciples out by having them pray with Him. Read Jesus' prayers in the Gospels and ask if this man was not earnestly involved in His praying. Our prayers may often go unanswered because we really care so little.

5. *Lack of Perseverance.* Closely related to earnestness is perseverance in prayer. Our lack of persistence may be one reason our prayers are not answered. We give up so easily. We pray once or twice, and then we're through. Some Christians will tell you that all you have to do is pray once about something, commit it to the Lord, and then relax and trust Him to take care of it. But I think I can say confidently that this is not the teaching of Jesus. Think of the parable of the friend coming at midnight to borrow some bread from his neighbor (Luke

11:5-8). The neighbor won't get up out of bed at first, but because his friend keeps pounding at the door and won't go away, he gets up and gives him the bread. How much more, says Jesus, will your heavenly Father give to you!

Or think of the parable of the widow and the judge (Luke 18:1-8). The unrighteous judge did not want to grant the woman's request, but she kept pestering him so much he said he would grant her request or else "she will wear me out by her continual coming" (18:5b, RSV). The point of the parable, says Luke, is that we "should always pray and not give up" (18:1). If we want something bad enough, we should beat a path to heaven's door and make its portals ring with our continual pounding. In Jan's and my own experience, some of our most dramatic answers to prayer—like getting a two-year fellowship from the West German government to study the evidence for the resurrection—have come as a response to prayers offered morning and evening over a period of several months.

I recently experienced a dramatic, unexpected answer to persistent prayer. Even since I became a Christian the evening of September 11, 1965, I have prayed that my unsaved parents would come to faith in Christ. Every day in my devotional time, five days a week, for over thirty years I prayed for their salvation—to no avail. It wasn't that they were hostile to Christ; they just didn't seem to feel any need of Him in their lives. Jan and I had shared the gospel with them several times and tried to live exemplary lives before them and spoke often of what God was doing in our own lives, but without any positive movement on my folks' part. I often wondered why God did so little in answer to my prayers for them. I would pray that He would bring someone or some influence for the gospel into their lives, but nothing much ever seemed to materialize. I figured that maybe God thought that He had already done so in giving them a son and daughter-in-law who were involved in Christian work. But I wished He would do more. So on and on I prayed, but frankly without much hope in the end of ever seeing a response to my prayers. A year ago last summer Jan and I were visiting my parents' home near Sedona, Arizona, where they had moved because the dry climate was beneficial for my father's

Parkinson's disease. Jan said to me, "You've got to speak to your Dad one more time about receiving Christ. Given how advanced his disease is, you may not ever have another chance." I knew she was right, but my heart really wasn't in it. It seemed such an exercise in futility. But I sat down with him in the living room and with a certain sense of awkwardness said, "You know, Dad, we really can't be sure how much longer you've got. You really need to be thinking about what happens when you go into eternity." His response floored me. "I don't really think there's any evidence for life beyond death," he said. I was flabbergasted! Here was a man who was about to die of a debilitating disease. You'd think he would be grasping at straws, any hope of immortality, no matter how implausible! Instead he was talking about evidence! On the one hand I must confess that I felt a sort of grudging respect for such disbelief. Here was in a sense unbelief with integrity: he wasn't going to believe just out of desperation. He wanted evidence. On the other hand, I also felt angry because he had never bothered to look at the evidence when he able to do so, and now he was so diminished in his capacities that he couldn't possibly investigate the evidence! I said, "Dad, I'm one of the world's leading experts on the historicity of Jesus' resurrection. I've been studying it for years, and you know the books I've written on the subject. His resurrection from the dead is the evidence for life beyond the grave and the basis for the Christian hope in eternal life. And I'm telling you, as an expert, that the historical evidence for Jesus' resurrection is very good. Unfortunately, you're too sick now to look at that evidence for yourself. So for you to come to Christ you're going to have to make two steps of faith. First of all, you going to have to trust Christ. Secondly, you're going to have to trust me."

He said he would think about it, and we left it at that. It was the same old brush-off, I thought. Then some weeks later Jan and I got a call at our home in Atlanta. It was my mother. "Your father's been thinking about what you told him," she said, "and he's ready to make that decision." You could have knocked me over with a feather! I couldn't believe my ears. All those years of praying for precisely this, and could it now really be? It didn't seem to be possible; it was unreal!

But we explained to her that on a particular page of one of my books which they owned there is a prayer of invitation to ask Christ into one's life as Savior and Lord. We explained to her how to pray through that prayer with my Dad and asked her to call us back once it was done. I couldn't believe this was really happening, but the next day she called us back. "We prayed the prayer together like you said. It took a long time because of your father's Parkinson's," she explained. "But we did it twice. I just want to be sure we're both going to the same place!"

I had received the marvelous answer to my persistent prayers. I also learned something through that experience. I realized that there had grown up in my heart an unknown root of bitterness toward God because of His seeming unresponsiveness to my prayers for my parents. All those years He seemed to be doing nothing. But now I came to appreciate what I, as a philosopher, had known intellectually for some time: that God may be at work providentially to accomplish His purposes in ways that we cannot even detect. He knew all along how to best answer my prayers, and I had only to be patient.[1] Don't give up too soon in your prayer for something. Show God that you mean business.

These, then, are some of the obstacles to answered prayer: *sin in our lives, wrong motives, lack of faith, lack of earnestness, lack of perseverance.* If any of those obstacles hinders our prayers, then we cannot claim with confidence Jesus' promise, "Whatever you ask in my name, I will do it" (John 14:13a, RSV).

But, of course, this isn't the end of the story. For the frustrating thing about unanswered prayer is that on occasion none of the obstacles just listed seems to impede the way, and still God does not grant our request. We may have confessed all known sin in our lives, prayed out of a desire to glorify God, and prayed in faith with earnestness and perseverance, and still God doesn't come through as Jesus said He would. Indeed, it is precisely when all those elements are pre-

---

[1] During the editing of this book, my father went to be with the Lord.

sent that the experience of unanswered prayer is apt to be devastating and demoralizing.

There is, however, one final, important qualification of Jesus' promise that needs to be made: our request must be in accordance with God's will. The apostle John makes this clear in 1 John 5:14-15: "This is the confidence we have in approaching God: that if we ask anything according to his will, he hears us. And if we know that he hears us—whatever we ask—we know that we have what we asked of him." It may well be the case that sometimes our prayers are not answered, not due to some fault of our own, but simply because God knows better than we do what ought to be done. Our perspective and wisdom are limited, but God's is the viewpoint of omniscience. He knows, as we do not, that sometimes it is better not to grant our requests.

Notice that John says our confidence is that if our prayers are in accordance with God's will, He will answer them. Therefore, we should always temper our prayers with the attitude "If it be Thy will." Now very often you hear it said that to pray "If it be Thy will" is a sort of namby-pamby, Milquetoast kind of prayer that shows a lack of boldness before God. I don't think the Scripture supports that assertion. John says that our confidence is not that God will answer our prayers, but that He will answer our prayers if they are in accordance with His will. Our degree of confidence that He will answer our prayers is proportional to our degree of confidence that they are His will. If we aren't sure our requests express His will, it is entirely proper to say, "If it be Thy will."

The decisive vindication of this way of praying is that this is the way Jesus prayed. In the Garden of Gethsemane He asked that God would avert the crucifixion, but then He added, "Yet not my will, but yours be done" (Luke 22:42). To ask for God's will is an expression of humility and submission to God. It is to acknowledge that He knows better than we do, and that we want His will even more than we want our request. When Paul prayed that God would heal him of his thorn in the flesh, God declined his request, saying, "My grace is sufficient for you, for my power is made perfect in weakness" (2 Cor. 12:9a). Paul's response? "I will boast all the more gladly about my weaknesses, so that Christ's power may rest upon me. That is why, for Christ's sake, I delight in weaknesses, in insults, in hardships, in persecutions, in difficulties. For when I am weak, then I am strong" (12:9b-10). Paul wanted to be healed, yes, but even more he wanted God's will for his life. Our attitude should be the same.

If we want our prayers to be answered, we should pray in accordance with God's will. But how do we know what sorts of things represent His will? Well, perhaps the best way to discern that is to read the prayers of the Bible to see what great men of God prayed for. I think we might be a little surprised. Read the prayers of Paul in his epistles, for example.

In *Ephesians,* Paul prayed:

> that God would give the Ephesians a spirit of wisdom in the knowledge of Himself;

> that they would know
>   the hope to which they had been called;
>   the riches of God's inheritance in the saints;
>   the greatness of God's power;

> that they would be strengthened through the Holy Spirit in the inner self;

> that Christ would dwell in their hearts by faith;

> that they, being rooted in love, would have the ability to know Christ's unfathomable love, so that they might be filled with all God's fullness.

In *Philippians,* Paul prayed:

> that the Philippians' love would abound more and more, coupled with knowledge and discernment, so that they would

approve what is excellent and be pure and blameless at Christ's return, filled with the fruits of righteousness.

In *Colossians,* Paul prayed:

> that the Colossians would be filled with the knowledge of God's will in all spiritual wisdom and understanding, so that they would lead a life worthy of the Lord, fully pleasing to Him, bearing fruit in every good work, and increasing in the knowledge of God.

In the letters to the *Thessalonians,* Paul asked:

> that the Lord would make the Thessalonians increase and abound in love toward one another and toward all men, so that they would be established unblamable in holiness at Christ's return;

> that the Lord would comfort their hearts and establish them in every good work and deed.

And in the letter to *Philemon,* Paul prayed:

> that the sharing of Philemon's faith would promote the knowledge of all the good that is ours in Christ.

Are *those* the kind of things we pray for? Why not?

I suspect that very often we are simply praying for the wrong things. What we desire is not what God desires, and so our prayers go askew. Our prayers will be answered only as our desires are brought into line with His.

Now two objections might be raised at this point. First, it might be said that we have so qualified Jesus' original promise that it has suffered death by a thousand qualifications. For there is an enormous difference between saying, "Whatever you ask in my name, I will do

it," and saying, "Whatever you ask in name, if you have no unconfessed sin in your life, and your motives are pure, and you have faith,
and you are really in earnest, and you persist in asking, and, to top it
all off, if it is God's will, then I will do it." I feel the force of this objection, but in the end I do not think it will stand. For I feel sure that
when Jesus made that original promise, He naturally presupposed the
qualifications we have just listed and would agree to them if we could
ask Him today. Indeed, most of those qualifications come from His
own teachings, as we have seen.

As for the stipulation concerning God's will, His blanket promise
is not incompatible with this qualification. For example, John, who
in 1 John 5:14 makes the qualification that prayer should be in accordance with God's will, made just a few paragraphs earlier a blanket
promise almost like the one Jesus made: "Dear friends, if our hearts
do not condemn us, we have confidence before God and receive from
him anything we ask, because we obey his commands and do what
pleases him" (1 John 3:21-22). Thus, in the course of a single letter
John says that if our lives are pleasing to God, we receive whatever
we ask (3:21-22), and that if we ask anything according to His will,
we receive whatever we ask (5:14). John did not think the qualification in 5:14 nullified the promise made in 3:21-22. Why should Jesus
have thought any differently?

And when you reflect on it, it would be a recipe for disaster for
God to simply give us whatever we ask. For we would always pray to
be delivered from any suffering or trial, and yet we know from
Scripture that suffering builds character and trials perfect our faith. If
God gave us whatever we asked, we would be immature, spoiled children, not men and women of God. On the other hand, I think John
may also be saying that as we keep Christ's commands and grow into
His likeness, our wills come to coincide more and more with God's
will, so that we can have confidence that whatever we ask we shall
receive. But even the most Christlike saint, even Christ Himself,
because of our limited perspective, must sometimes pray, "Not my
will, but Thine be done."

A second objection is to say that when we pray, "Thy will be done," Jesus' promise to answer our prayers becomes unfalsifiable. That is to say, there is no way to tell if His promise is really true, for anytime we pray for something and do not receive it, we can always say, "It wasn't God's will"! Therefore, the promise seems empty. But this objection betrays a lack of understanding as to how we know that our Christian faith is true. Our confidence in the truth of Christianity in general and Jesus' promise in particular is not based on the evidence of answered prayer. Our confidence in the truth of our faith is based on the witness of the Holy Spirit, confirmed by reason. Prayer is one of the dimensions of the life of faith, not of apologetics. The Christian life is a walk by faith, and it is strictly irrelevant whether God's promises are falsifiable or not. The point is, we think Christianity is true (or presumably we wouldn't have become Christians), and so we place our trust in God's promises. Consequently, the objection is based on a misunderstanding of the basis of Christian faith.

But if there are no objections to this understanding of prayer and God's will, there is still a real danger here, which I have experienced, namely, timidity in prayer. That is to say, because we are uncertain of God's will in a specific situation, we do not know what to pray for. So we are afraid to ask God for something, lest we be praying outside of His will. If a friend is sick, should we pray that God heal him or that God give him courage and faith in his suffering? If we are unemployed, should we pray for a job or for an attitude of contentment as we learn to be abased? If someone is going through a trial, should we pray for deliverance or for steadfastness? We can be so cowed by not knowing what to pray for that we cease to pray, which is certainly not God's will. What are we supposed to do?

Well, praise be to God, there is a ministry of the Holy Spirit especially suited to this problem! Paul addresses precisely this problem in Romans 8:26-27: "In the same way, the Spirit helps us in our weakness. We do not know what we ought to pray for, but the Spirit himself intercedes for us with groans that words cannot express. And he who searches our hearts knows the mind of the Spirit, because the Spirit intercedes for the saints in accordance with God's will." We may not know what to pray for, but the Holy Spirit takes our prayers and translates them, as it were, into accordance with God's will before the throne of grace. With such a divine intercessor, we can pray boldly, even within our limited perspective, confident that the Holy Spirit is interceding according to the will of God. Therefore, be bold in your prayers and ask Him forthrightly for what you, using your spiritual wisdom and discernment, think best. That was also Paul's procedure. He boldly asked God to heal him, and he frequently asked the churches to pray for his deliverance from his persecutors, though in the end God had a different will for Paul. Pray according to your wisdom and your heart's desire, and trust the Holy Spirit to intercede for you according to the will of God.

In conclusion, I think it is obvious that this discussion has enormous practical implications for our lives. For although we have concentrated on unanswered prayer, since it is problematic, it is clear from Jesus' promise that unanswered prayer ought to be the exception, not the norm, of our prayer life. For the Christian abiding in Christ, answers to his prayers ought to be his regular experience. Now, how about your prayer life? Are you just muddling along in the Christian life, never seeing God really work in response to your prayers? When was the last time you moved the hands of God through prayer?

If you are not satisfied with your prayer life, maybe it's time to take inventory of the obstacles to answered prayer in your life. What is that unconfessed sin, that area of uncleanness in your life you've been rationalizing away or hiding from God? What room in your heart has not yet been opened to Christ and yielded to His lordship? Have you been praying just for selfish things that you might spend your passions on them? Or are you really seeking God's glory? Are you really believing God for answers to your prayers? Or have you become so accustomed to lack of answers that you've been lulled into a spiritual lethargy that expects no answer and so gets no answer from God? Do you really care whether He answers or not? Do you go to God with an intense, burning desire to have your requests from Him? Do you pray once and forget about it, or do you come to God again and again?

Do you wrestle with God, saying with Jacob, "I will not let you go unless you bless me" (Gen. 32:26b)? In a word, do you pray because that's what Christians are expected to do, or do you mean business with God?

If you do mean business, let me make this suggestion: set aside some time tomorrow—or even today—to take inventory of the hindrances to prayer in your life. Repent, ask God's forgiveness, and start anew. Make out a prayer list of specific people and things to pray for on different days of the week, and then set aside time to pray each day for these. Be specific, and put a red check by each request as it is answered. As you see God work, your faith will increase as you learn to trust Him for more.

If you already have a vital prayer life but have been troubled by certain unanswered prayers, you need to trust God for His perfect will. Reflect on His omniscience and His goodness. If you ask Him for bread, will He give you a stone? (Matt. 7:9). If you ask for a fish, will He give you a scorpion? (Luke 11: 12). God will give to you what His good and acceptable and perfect will decrees. You may not always get what you ask for, but God knows best what will serve to advance His kingdom. You can trust Him for His answers. Prayer is hard work. But the promises of prayer are great. Let us therefore strive to lay hold of those promises.

3

FAILURE

I have been a Christian for more than thirty years. I estimate that in my Christian lifetime I have attended upward of a couple of thousand church services, hundreds of chapels at Wheaton College, and scores of Christian meetings at retreats, conferences, and so on, held by Campus Crusade and other groups. Yet during this entire time I have never once—not a single time in the thousands of meetings over some thirty-odd years—heard a speaker address the subject of failure. In fact, I probably would not myself have reflected seriously on the topic if it had not been for a crushing failure that drove me to face the problem personally.

The lack of treatment of this subject on the part of Christian speakers is not due to any lack of importance in the subject. Any Christian who has failed at some time knows how devastating the experience can be and the questions it raises: *Where is God? How could He let this happen? Am I outside of His will? What do I do now? Does God really care, or even exist?* Those are agonizing questions. What is the meaning of failure for a Christian?

In addressing this problem, it seems to me that we need first to distinguish two types of failure: *failure in the Christian life* and *failure in the life of a Christian.* By failure in the Christian life, I mean a failure in a believer's relationship and walk with God. For example, a Christian might experience disappointment and failure due to a refusal to heed God's calling, or by succumbing to temptation, or through marrying a non-Christian. Failure of this type is due to sin. It is essentially a spiritual problem, a matter of moral and spiritual failure.

By contrast, failure in the life of a Christian is unrelated to spiritual considerations. It is not due to sin in the life of a believer. It is just some defeat a person who happens to be a Christian experiences in his day-to-day life. For example, a Christian businessman might go bankrupt, a Christian athlete might see his boyhood dreams shattered when he fails to make the major leagues, a Christian student might flunk out of school despite his best efforts to succeed, or a Christian workingman might find himself unemployed and unable to find a job. Such cases are not instances of failure in a person's walk with God but instances of failure in the ordinary course of life. They just happen to occur in the lives of people who are Christians.

In his best-selling book *Failure: The Back Door to Success,* Erwin Lutzer deals with the distinction I am trying to make here. He attributes failure in the Christian life to lust of the flesh (sexual gratification), pride of life (egoism), or lust of the eyes (covetousness). Failure in the life of a Christian that is not related to those elements is just part of life. Lutzer finds no particular difficulty with the second type of failure, but he does find the first kind of failure problematic. He writes:

> What causes failure? What makes a man come to the end of his life and admit he lived in vain? What motivates a man to commit suicide because he is not as gifted as others? . . . What causes a man to jeopardize his Christian testimony and have an affair with his neighbor's wife? The answer: Sin—specifically, pride, covetousness, or sensual desire.
>
> Of course, there are failures quite unrelated to sinful motivations: a student might fail in school, a man might make an unwise investment. Many people have failed at their jobs or simply fallen short of their goals. We shouldn't minimize this type of failure, but in the long run it is not as serious as spiritual failure.[1]

---

[1] Erwin Lutzer, *Failure: The Back Door to Success* (Chicago: Moody, 1975), 41-42.

Lutzer devotes his entire book to failure in the Christian life, the first kind of failure, because he thinks that kind of failure has more serious consequences than the second type of failure. In one sense, that is true: one is morally guilty for failure due to sin. Failure in the Christian life breaks one's fellowship with God and has eternal consequences. We need to confess this type of failure to God, or we shall be held accountable and judged for it. So in the ultimate sense, the consequences of failure in the Christian life are far more serious than the ordinary failures that happen to occur in our lives.

On the other hand, however, in terms of everyday consequences in the world in which we live, it is not always true that the first type of failure has the more serious consequences. For if we do not know how to respond properly to it, failure in the life of a Christian can be even more devastating than failure that comes about specifically because of our sin.

Now I have no particular difficulty in understanding failure in the Christian life. Of course, sin leads to failure! What else could we expect? Nor is the solution to this sort of failure difficult to understand: repentance, confession, faith, and obedience. So I do not find failure in the Christian life puzzling, especially when I reflect on the weakness of my own flesh. It is not surprising that we sin and fail.

But the second type of failure is problematic to me. When someone is walking in faith and obedience to the Lord, how can he be led into the pit of failure? Think about it. How can obeying God's will lead to failure? This is, indeed, puzzling. Therefore, I want to focus our attention on this second kind of failure, failure in the life of a Christian, and see if we can come to understand it.

For many years I had the point of view that Christians who are walking in God's will basically cannot fail. Perhaps I was just outrageously naive, but I don't think so. I had given the matter serious thought and had even qualified my position at several important points. For example, I distinguished failure from persecution. Scripture is clear that those who are trying to live godly lives in Christ Jesus will experience persecution, and Jesus said that they will be blessed for it (see 2 Tim. 3:12; Matt. 5:10-12). Christians who have died in concentration camps because of their faith, or who have lost jobs or been discriminated against because they were Christians, could not properly be said to have failed.

I also distinguished failure from trials. The Scripture is clear that as Christians we are not exempt from trials and that such testing produces maturity and endurance. Without trials we would remain pampered and spoiled children. But I believed that if we endured our trials in reliance upon God's strength, He would see us through and bring us victoriously to the other side. Basically, it just did not make sense to me to say that God would call a person to do something and then—when that person was obedient to the call and was relying on God's strength—allow him to fail.

And, in fact, there is some scriptural support for the position I took. Look at what Psalm 1:1-3 says:

> Blessed is the man
>   who does not walk in the counsel of the wicked
> or stand in the way of sinners
>   or sit in the seat of mockers.
> But his delight is in the law of the LORD,
>   and on his law he meditates day and night.
> He is like a tree planted by streams of water,
>   which yields its fruit in season
> and whose leaf does not wither.
>   Whatsoever he does prospers.

What could be clearer? In all that he does, he prospers! But then I experienced a disastrous personal failure that forced me to rethink this entire issue. It occurred while Jan and I were living in West Germany and I was finishing my doctoral studies in theology at the University of Munich under the famous theologian Wolfhart Pannenberg. My dissertation had already been approved, and all that remained was to pass the oral examination in theology (ominously called the *Rigorosum*). Not knowing what to expect, I tried repeatedly to get an appointment with Pannenberg to discuss the examination and how I might prepare for it. But I was never able to see him (German professors tend to be much more reclusive than their American counterparts). So I went to his teaching assistant, a brilliant young theologian who had earned his doctorate under Pannenberg. He brushed aside the idea of preparing for the examination. "Forget it!" he advised. Well, I wasn't that stupid, so I pressed him further on how I might prepare. "Pannenberg always asks questions only over his own writings," he responded. "Just read what he has written."

That seemed to me to be a good strategy, and so over the next several weeks I read and studied virtually everything Pannenberg had ever written. I felt confident that I had mastered his thought.

On the day of the examination I entered Pannenberg's office. He would deliver the exam himself, and the process was to be monitored and recorded by the dean of the theology faculty and one other professor of theology. We shook hands all around and sat down for the questioning to commence.

Almost immediately things began to go wrong. Pannenberg began to ask questions on subjects that were not discussed in his writings. He began to ask about the particularities of this or that man's theology. And I could not answer the questions. Again and again I had to confess my ignorance. I cannot convey to you the feeling of helplessness and fear that swept over me. Question after question, I realized that I was watching my doctorate slip away before me, and—like trying to grasp sand slipping through your fingers—there was nothing I could do to stop it. This torture went on for nearly an hour. Near the end of the hour's examination, just to make my failure patently evident to all, Pannenberg asked a couple of condescendingly easy questions, as if to come down to my level of knowledge. My humiliation was complete.

Devastated, I left the theology department to meet Jan to go out to dinner at a restaurant where the two of us had planned to celebrate. She came rushing up to me, smiling, with a look of expectancy in her eyes. "Honey, I failed," I said. She couldn't believe it. It was just before Christmas, and on the twenty-third we had planned to fly back to the

United States to visit my family and begin teaching at Trinity Evangelical Divinity School in Deerfield, Illinois. Now we were going home in defeat. As if to add injury to insult, on the flight back Lufthansa lost our IBM typewriter, Jan's handbag where she had packed her most valuable personal effects was stolen, and I lost both of my contact lenses!

But those material losses were nothing compared to the turmoil I felt inside over losing my doctorate. I just couldn't understand how God could have let it happen. He had called us to Germany and miraculously supplied the finances for my study. We were walking in His will; I was sure of it. I had not been negligent or overconfident. I had tried often to see Pannenberg in advance, but he was always too busy for me, so I prepared the best way I knew how. But especially, we had prayed earnestly and faithfully for this examination, and there were others, Spirit-filled Christians in the United States, praying for it, too. The examination had been entirely fair, I couldn't deny that. I had just failed it, that's all. But how could God have let it happen? What about His promises? "In all that he does, he prospers." "Whatsoever you ask in my name . . ."

It wasn't just that I had failed an examination. More than that, my failure was a spiritual crisis in faith for me. I felt hurt and disgraced, but even more, I felt betrayed by God. How could I ever trust Him again?

As I worked through my feelings in the ensuing days, it became clear to me that Psalm 1:1-3 just could not be construed as some sort of blanket promise that covers every case. Christians don't always prosper in what they undertake. Sometimes they do fail, and that's just a fact.

Now someone might say, "You can't use human experience to nullify God's Word! His promises stand regardless of your experience." But the problem with this response is that Scripture itself gives examples of such failure. For instance, God had promised to give the land of Canaan to the twelve tribes of Israel. But in Judges 1:19 we read, "The Lord was with the men of Judah. They took possession of the hill country, but they were unable to drive the people from the plains, because they had iron chariots." Look at what it says here: *the Lord was with the armies of Judah*—but despite that fact, although they conquered the hill country, they failed to defeat their enemy in the plains because they had iron chariots! It doesn't seem to make sense: God was with them, and yet they failed. How are we to understand such failure in the life of the believer?

Now some people might answer that question by claiming that God has no specific will for our lives. God's will is His general desire that we obey His ethical and spiritual commands, that we arrive at a Christlike character, and so forth. But He has no specific will for individual persons that includes such matters as getting a doctorate, marrying a certain person, or entering into a particular business deal. So when we undertake those things, we do so wholly on our own initiative and may well wind up in failure.

But this solution strikes me as inadequate, despite its apparent appeal to many people. In the first place, it implies a deficient concept of God's sovereignty, providence, and guidance. Although the Bible teaches human freedom, it also has a strong emphasis on God's sovereign control and providential direction over everything that happens. Nothing happens in the world without God's directly willing it, or, in the case of sinful acts, at least permitting it. Moreover, God has so providentially ordered the world that His ends will be accomplished by the things we decide to undertake. Our decisions, then, cannot be a matter of indifference to Him. Moreover, He has promised to guide us in what we decide. All this suggests that God does have a specific will for our lives.

But that point aside, in the second place, this proposed solution doesn't actually get to the heart of the problem. For even if God does not have a specific will for our lives, the fact remains that He has promised to be with us, empowering and helping us. That is why the example in Judges is so puzzling. The Lord was with them, but still they failed. So even if God has no specific will for our lives, that still doesn't explain how we can fail in things we decide to do in His strength.

And so I was led to what was, for me, a radical new insight into the will of God, namely, that God's *will for our lives can include failure.* In other words, God's will may be that you fail, and He may lead you into failure! For there are things that God has to teach you through failure that He could never teach you through success.

In my own case, failing my doctoral exams forced me to see my life's priorities in a new light. When we returned to my folks for Christmas, I broke the news to my parents that I had failed my oral examination and didn't receive the doctorate. To my astonishment, my mother retorted, "Who cares?" I was stunned! To me it seemed like the catastrophe of a lifetime, but she just shrugged it off as though it didn't matter. It dawned on me that in one sense it really didn't, that there are things in life a good deal more important than doctorates, publications, and academic fame. In the end, it was human relationships that really mattered—especially family relationships.

My mind went back to a scientist we had met in Germany who had been divorced for many years and who wanted with all his heart to return to his wife and little boy. "When I was first married," he had told us, "I spent all my time in the laboratory. All I could think of was my research to the exclusion of anything or anyone else." It had seemed so important to him then. But now he knew it wasn't. "I was a fool," he said. And so I, too, now realized afresh the blessings I had in a faithful wife who had sacrificed and worked with me all those years I was in school, and in loving parents who accepted me unconditionally just because I was their son. That Christmas marked the beginning of a new relationship with my folks. Jan and I have come to know them not merely as parents but as friends.

You see, I had failed to understand what true success really is. True success is not achieving wealth, power, or fame. True success lies in the realm of the spiritual, or to be more specific, lies in getting to know God better. J. I. Packer expresses this thought succinctly in *Knowing God:*

> We have been brought to the point where we both can and must get our life's priorities straight. From current Christian publications you might think that the most vital issue for any real or would-be

Christian in the world today is church union, or social witness, or dialogue with other Christians and other faiths, or refuting this or that -ism, or developing a Christian philosophy and culture, or what have you. But our line of study makes the present-day concentration on these things look like a gigantic conspiracy of misdirection. Of course, it is not that; the issues themselves are real and must be dealt with in their place. But it is tragic that, in paying attention to them, so many in our day seem to have been distracted from what was, is, and always will be the true priority for every human being— that is, learning to know God in Christ.[2]

When I first read this statement, it took me aback: "refuting this or that -ism or developing a Christian philosophy." Exactly the sort of thing I am about in life! And yet it is not the most important. One could succeed in it and yet, in God's sight, still be a failure.

That brings to mind a thought that Lutzer says came to haunt him as a busy pastor: *You may not be accomplishing as much as you think you are.* We can be doing many things for the Lord and still fail to be the kind of person God desires us to be. Indeed, my greatest fear is that I should some day stand before the Lord and see all my works go up in smoke like so much "wood, hay, and stubble" (see 1 Cor. 3:12, KJV). What, after all, did Jesus say? "Many who are first will be last, and many who are last will be first" (Matt. 19:30). It is not success in the eyes of the world that ultimately counts, but success in the Lord's eyes.

Now this is both encouraging and convicting. On the one hand, it is encouraging because even though we fail, failure may be the better part of success in the Lord's eyes. I have a hunch that God is not so much interested in what we go through as in how we go through it. Though we may fail in the task that we've set out to do, if we respond to that failure with faith, courage, and dependency on the Lord's strength, rather than with despair, bitterness, and depression, we are counted a success in His sight.

On the other hand, it is convicting because we may think that we are accomplishing a lot when actually we are failing in the Lord's

[2] J. I. Packer, *Knowing God* (London: Hodder & Stoughton, 1973), 314.

sight. The apostle Paul recognized that he could be a brilliant and gifted theologian, one who lived in poverty because of his generosity and who was even martyred for preaching the gospel, and yet, if he lacked love, be nothing in God's sight (1 Cor. 13:1-3). For true success is found in loving God and your fellow man.

Well, what practical application does all this have for our lives? Two points can be made.

First, we need to learn from our failures. When we fail, we shouldn't adopt the sour grapes attitude of the fox in Aesop's fable. Instead, we should analyze our failure to see what lesson we can learn from it. That doesn't mean trying to figure out why God allowed it to happen. In many cases, we'll never know why. Too many Christians fall into what Packer calls the "York signal box mistake."[3] In the train yards in the city of York is a master control room containing an electronic panel showing in lights the position of every train in the yard. Someone in the control tower, who sees the whole panel, can understand just why a particular train was put on hold at one spot or why another was shunted into a siding somewhere else, even though to someone down on the tracks the movements of the trains may appear to be inexplicable. The Christian who wants to know why God permits every failure in his life is asking, Packer says, to be in God's "signal box," and yet, for better or for worse, we just don't have access to it. Therefore, it is pointless to torture ourselves about why God permitted this or that disaster to come into our lives.

But although we don't always discern or comprehend God's providential design, we can still learn from our failures. As Lutzer says, "It isn't necessary to know why God sent us the misfortune in order to profit from it."[4] Ask yourself what you should have done differently in your situation or what you could do differently next time. Ask yourself what sort of reaction God wants you to have, or what character trait can be developed in you as a result of the defeat. Learn from your failure.

---

[3] Ibid., 110-111.
[4] Lutzer, *Failure,* 66.

Second, never give up. Just because you have failed, it's not all over for you. Here the example of a man like Richard Nixon is instructive. Narrowly defeated by John F. Kennedy in the 1960 presidential election, Nixon returned to his home state of California only to fail again in his bid for the governorship. It looked like his political career was over. "You won't have Dick Nixon to kick around anymore," he grumped to the press. But quietly he was laying the groundwork for a comeback. In 1968 he beat Hubert Humphrey for the presidency and in 1972 crushed his challenger George McGovern. Then came Watergate. Disgraced and facing impeachment, he ignominiously resigned the office of president. No one, I dare say, ever expected to hear much from him again.

But a few years later, there he was speaking at the Oxford University Debating Union and arguing on issues of public policy. He continued to do so, and a few years later *Newsweek* magazine ran a cover story on Nixon. On the front of the magazine, beside his picture, was the simple statement in large yellow letters, "He's Back!" It summed up the fact that Nixon had come to be regarded as something of an elder statesman whose foreign policy opinions and shrewd political advice were much sought after.

When Nixon was asked at Oxford to explain the secret of his surprising comeback, he gave this advice, which we would do well to take to heart: "You're never through when you fail. You're only through when you quit. Never quit. Never, never, never."

That's good advice. You're not finished just because you fail. You're only finished if you give up and quit. But don't quit! With God's strength, pick up the pieces of your failure and, having learned from it, go on.

That's what we did in our case, and I'm glad to say that the story has a happy ending. At German universities, if you fail the oral examinations the first time, you can retake them. Jan and I both knew that I had to try again, and our friends encouraged us to do so. So after beginning to teach at Trinity seminary, I spent the next entire year preparing again for the *Rigorosum*. I worked through Harnack's prodigious three-volume *Dogmengeschichte,* Pelikan's multi-volume *History of the Development of Doctrine,* Cunliffe-Jones's *History of Christian Doctrine,* Loof's *Dogmengeschichte,* two lengthy study guides on the whole of Dogmatics prepared for German university students in theology, as well as studying the documents of the various councils and creeds of the church, readings in the church fathers, works on contemporary theology, and so forth. By the time the year was out, I had a stack of notes about a foot high, which I had virtually memorized, and was prepared to answer questions on any area of systematic theology—be it Christology, anthropology, soteriology, or whatever—from the early Apologists to the Middle Ages, through the Reformation, the Enlightenment, and the twentieth century. I was set. But I was scared to death.

When I walked into Pannenberg's office, everything looked pretty much the same as before. But this time, it was different. Pannenberg began with the doctrine of the Trinity, starting with the logos doctrine of the early Apologists. And to my joy (which I could scarcely conceal!), as the examination continued to unfold, I found myself readily responding to each question with full and accurate answers. The only question I tripped up on was one about why Hegel's doctrine of the incarnation entailed the death of God—and I didn't feel so bad about missing that one! Pannenberg himself was clearly delighted with my success and awarded me a *magna cum laude* for the examination. I was dancing on air!

So it was a victory for the Lord in the end. But the victory was not just in passing the examination. For, not to mention the spiritual lessons God taught me, I discovered a sobering truth. Like so many other American students, I had been woefully trained in seminary in the history of Christian doctrine. The training in systematic theology that American evangelical seminaries generally give their students is but a pale shadow of what German university students in theology receive. Is it therefore any wonder that skeptical German theology leads the world? How can we ever hope that evangelical theology will become a leading model unless we begin to train our students with the same rigor and thoroughness that characterize German theological instruction? I can say without hesitation that during that year of intense study I learned more about systematic theology than I did during my entire seminary training. So although I would never want to relive my experience, I can honestly say that I'm glad I failed the exam the first time around. It was for the best, because as a result of that failure I became theologically equipped for the Lord's service in a way that would never have been possible if I had passed.

And I'm so glad that we didn't quit. Suppose we had just given up. Let's say that in the humiliation of my failure, I had lost hope and not tried to take the exam the second time. The pangs of defeat would have haunted me every time I thought of my failure or opened a book on systematic theology. I would not have had that year of intensive study, and I would have remained in my anemic state of theological knowledge. The years would have passed, and I would have continually asked myself the question: *Should I have tried again?* Even if I had tried and failed the second time, I would still have been better off than by quitting. To paraphrase an old motto in a different context: It is better to have tried and failed than not to have tried at all.

So when you encounter failure, don't give up. Ask God for the strength to go on. He will give it to you. In fact, there is a biblical name for that quality. It is called *endurance*. Through failure, if you respond correctly, God can build the quality of endurance into your life.

Failure in the life of a Christian, then, should not surprise us. God has important things to teach us through failure—and true success, the success that counts for eternity, consists in learning those lessons. So when you fail, do not despair or think that God has abandoned you; rather, learn from your failures and never give up. That is the formula for success.

4

SUFFERING AND
EVIL (1)

Undoubtedly the greatest intellectual obstacle to belief in God—for both the Christian and the non-Christian—is the so-called problem of evil. That is to say, it seems unbelievable that if an all-powerful and all-loving God exists, He would permit so much pain and suffering in the world.

The amount of human misery and pain in the world is, indeed, incalculable. On the one hand, there are all the evils that are the result of man's own inhumanity to man. Unlike the beasts, man seems to have a penchant for almost unimaginable cruelty to others. Perhaps the most forceful way to bring this home is to read a book such as Daniel P. Mannix's *History of Torture*[1] or to visit a medieval castle and look at the terrible devices used to inflict pain on prisoners. What is especially sickening is that historically the church has been part of this barbarism. Between 1096 and 1274, for example, the medieval church launched eight major Crusades, as well as numerous smaller ventures, aimed at liberating the Holy Land from Islamic control. These expeditions, which were characterized by greed, deceit, and the lust for power, accomplished almost nothing and resulted in the loss of thousands of lives. The fourth Crusade, for example, launched in

---

[1] Daniel P. Mannix, *History of Torture* (Stroud, Gloucestershire, England: Sutton, 2003).

1204, was supposed to be aimed at Egypt, but at the last minute the Crusaders diverted the mission and sacked instead the Christian city of Zara and then attacked Constantinople, the capital of the eastern Christian empire, pillaging the city with what one historian described as "unparalleled horrors." But the most heinous of these expeditions was the so-called Children's Crusade of 1212. In this ludicrous mission, thousands of children were recruited to form an army to liberate the Holy Land. But the children never got any farther than Marseille, France. There they were kidnapped and sold into slavery by the leaders of the Crusade.

The history of mankind is a history of bloodshed and war. Some years ago on PBS I saw a ten-part serial, "The World at War," which presented a history of the Second World War. The last installment of the program calculated the lives lost in that conflict: 6 million Jews slain in Nazi concentration camps, 16 million lives lost in Germany, 20 million persons killed in the Soviet Union, and so on. The numbers were staggering. In all, some 51 million people were killed in World War II. Think of it! And that says nothing of the millions and millions of wounded, of the untold suffering of the living, of the poverty, starvation, dehumanization, immorality, and disruption of normal lives that war throws up in its wake. And lest those statistics numb us by their inconceivability, we ought to remind ourselves that those people died *one at a time.*

Perhaps no one has stated more powerfully the objection that human, moral evil poses to the existence of God than the great Russian novelist Fyodor Dostoyevsky. In a scene in the novel *The Brothers Karamazov* the atheist Ivan explains to his brother Alyosha, a Russian Orthodox priest, how evil in the world makes it impossible for him to believe in God:

> "By the way, a Bulgarian I met lately in Moscow," Ivan went on, seeming not to hear his brother's words, "told me about the crimes committed by Turks and Circassians in all parts of Bulgaria through fear of a general rising of the Slavs. . . . People talk sometimes of bestial cruelty, but that's a great injustice and insult to the beast; a beast

can never be so cruel as a man, so artistically cruel. . . . These Turks took a pleasure in torturing children, too; cutting the unborn child from the mother's womb, and tossing babies up in the air and catching them on the points of their bayonets before their mother's eyes. Doing it before the mother's eyes was what gave zest to the amusement. Here is another scene that I thought very interesting. Imagine a trembling mother with her baby in her arms, a circle of invading Turks around her. They've planned a diversion: they pet the baby, laugh to make it laugh. They succeed, the baby laughs. At that moment a Turk points a pistol four inches from the baby's face. The baby laughs with glee, holds out its little hands to the pistol, and he pulls the trigger in the baby's face and blows out its brains. Artistic, wasn't it. . . .

"But I've still better things about children. I've collected a great, great deal about Russian children, Alyosha. There was a little girl of five who was hated by her father and mother, most worthy and respectable people, of good education and breeding. . . . This poor child of five was subjected to every possible torture by those cultivated parents. They beat her, thrashed her, kicked her for no reason till her body was one bruise. Then, they went to greater refinements of cruelty—shut her up all night in the cold and frost in a privy, and because she didn't ask to be taken up at night (as though a child of five sleeping its angelic, sound sleep could be trained to wake and ask), they smeared her face and filled her mouth with excrement, and it was her mother, her mother did this. And that mother could sleep, hearing the poor child's groans! Can you understand why a little creature, who can't even understand what's done to her, should beat her little aching heart with her tiny fist in the dark and the cold, and weep her meek unresentful tears to dear, kind God to protect her? . . . Do you understand why this infamy must be and is permitted? Without it, I am told, man could not have lasted on earth, for he could not have known good and evil. Why should he know that diabolical good and evil when it costs so much? Why, the whole world of knowledge is not worth that child's prayer to dear, kind God!"[2]

---

[2] Fyodor Dostoyevsky, *The Brothers Karamazov,* trans. Constance Garnett (New York: New American Library, 1957), 219-223.

Such moral evil is bad enough, but perhaps even more difficult to reconcile with the existence of an all-powerful and loving God is the suffering brought on by natural causes in the world. One thinks of natural disasters, such as floods, earthquakes, or tornadoes; of the different sorts of diseases, such as smallpox, polio, cancer, or leukemia; of congenital disabilities, such as muscular dystrophy, cerebral palsy, or encephalitis; of accidents and injuries, such as being burned, drowning, or falling. Sometimes these natural evils are intertwined with human evils: for example, there are countries in which millions face starvation, not because there are not enough relief supplies to meet the need, but because the government will not permit those supplies to reach the people but instead uses food as a political weapon to crush rebel resistance.

In 1985 the horror of natural evils was brought home to me in a powerful way through two incidents shown on television. In Mexico City a terrible earthquake had devastated blocks of high-rise apartment buildings. As rescue teams in the aftermath of the quake searched the rubble for survivors, they came across a ten-year-old boy who was trapped alive somewhere in the recesses of a collapsed building. During the next several days, the whole world watched in agony as the teams tried to remove the rubble to get to the boy. They could communicate with him, but could not reach him. His grandfather, who had been trapped with him, was already dead. "I'm scared!" he cried. After about eleven days, there was silence. Alone in the darkness, trapped without food, afraid, the little boy died before the rescue teams could free him.

That same year a mudslide swept over a village in Colombia. As rescuers came to help survivors, they came across a little girl who was pinned up to her chin in muddy water. For some reason or other, they could not free her or remove the water. All they could do was stand by helplessly and watch her die. Every night on the news we saw films of the little girl's decline. It was the most pathetic sight I have ever seen. She stood there, unable to move, spitting out the water that continually flowed into her mouth. As the days went by, she became more exhausted, and deep, black circles formed under her eyes. She was dying before our very eyes, as we watched on television. Finally, the evening newscaster reported that she was gone.

Those two incidents rent my heart. *Oh, God!* I thought. *How could You permit those children to die like that? If they had to die, so be it! But You could have let the boy be killed instantly by the collapse of the building or let the little girl drown suddenly. Why these torturous pointless, lingering deaths?* I'll be honest with you. When I see these sorts of things go on, it makes it hard to believe in God.

When I was a very young Christian, I thought that such things didn't happen to Christians who were walking in God's will. Didn't Romans 8:28 say that "we know that in all things God works for the good of those who love him, who have been called according to his purpose"? Christians who experienced pointless, gratuitous suffering must have strayed from God's will. But such a naive outlook is obviously incorrect, for the righteous and innocent *do* suffer. I think of a prominent Christian leader in my home town who was decapitated in a sledding accident when he ran into a barbed wire fence he hadn't seen; or of a pastor who backed out of his driveway and ran over his infant son, who had been playing behind the car; or of some Canadian missionaries who were forced to return from the field when their little daughter fell from her third-story window to the concrete driveway below and suffered severe brain damage. Clearly, Christians have not been exempted from the apparently pointless evils of the world.

In light of the quantity and nature of the suffering brought on by human or natural causes, how can it be that an all-powerful, all-good God exists? This is a question that must trouble many people, for several years ago Rabbi Harold Kushner was able to make his book a best-seller by titling it *When Bad Things Happen to Good People.*[3] Unfortunately, he could not solve the problem, for he could answer the question only by denying that God is all-powerful. But if we stick with the biblical conception of God, how are we to account for the existence of evil in a world that was made and is sustained by an all-powerful, all-good God?

---

[3] Harold Kushner, *When Bad Things Happen to Good People* (Boston: G. K. Hall, 1981).

Let me begin by making a number of distinctions to help us to keep our thinking straight. In the first place, we must distinguish between the intellectual problem of evil and the emotional problem of evil. The *intellectual* problem of evil concerns how to give a rational explanation of God and evil. The *emotional* problem of evil concerns how to comfort or console those who are suffering and how to dissolve the emotional dislike people have of a God who would permit such evil. The intellectual problem is in the province of the philosopher; the emotional problem is in the province of the counselor. It is important to understand this distinction, because the solution to the intellectual problem is apt to appear dry, uncaring, and uncomforting to someone who is going through suffering, whereas the solution to the emotional problem is apt to appear deficient as an explanation of evil to someone contemplating it abstractly.

Keeping this distinction in mind, let us turn first to the intellectual problem of evil.

Here again, we need to make a distinction. There are two ways of formulating the intellectual problem of evil, either as an *internal* problem or as an *external* problem. That is to say, the problem may be presented as arising from certain beliefs to which Christians are committed in virtue of being Christians, so that the Christian worldview is somehow at odds with itself. On the other hand, the problem may be presented in terms of truths to which Christians are not committed as Christians but which we nonetheless have good reason to believe. The first approach tries to expose an inner tension within the Christian worldview itself; the second approach attempts to present evidence against the truth of the Christian worldview.

Now the internal problem of evil takes two forms: the *logical* version and the *probabilistic* version. In the logical version of the problem, the atheist's goal is to show that it is logically impossible for both God and evil to exist, just as it is logically inconsistent to say that an irresistible force and an immovable object both exist. The two are logically incompatible. If one exists, the other does not. The Christian faith is committed to the reality of evil, just as it is to the reality of an omnipotent and omnibenevolent God. But this is inconsistent. Since we know that evil exists, the argument goes, it follows logically that God must not exist.

In the probabilistic version of the problem, the admission is made that it is possible that God and evil coexist, but it is insisted that such a coexistence of God and evil is highly improbable. Thus, the Christian theist is stuck with two beliefs which tend to undermine each other. Given that the evil in the world is real, it is highly improbable that God exists.

We can graphically display these distinctions as follows:

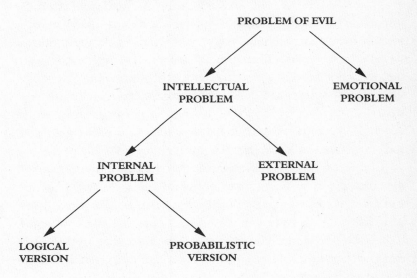

Let us examine each of these versions of the argument in turn. We shall consider first the *internal problem of evil*. As we have noted, this version of the problem holds that the two statements "An all-powerful, all-good God exists" and "Evil exists" are logically inconsistent. They cannot both be true.

Now at face value, those statements are not inconsistent. There is not an explicit contradiction between them. But if the atheist means that there is some implicit contradiction between them, he must be assuming some hidden premises that would serve to bring out the contradiction and make it explicit. But what are those assumptions?

There seem to be two: (1) if God is all-powerful, then He can create any world that He chooses, and (2) if God is all-good, then He would prefer a world without evil over a world with evil. The atheist reasons that since God is all-powerful, He could create a world containing free creatures who always freely choose to do right. Such a world would be a sinless world, free of all human, moral evils. By the same token, being all-powerful, God could as well create a world in which no natural evils ever occurred. It would be a world free of evil, pain, and suffering.

Now notice that the atheist is not saying that men would be mere puppets in such a world. No, he's saying that it's possible for a world to exist in which everyone *freely* makes the right decision. Such a world must be possible from the Christian point of view, for if it were not, we would be saying that sin is necessary, which would be unbiblical. Thus whenever a moral decision is made, it is theoretically possible always to decide to do the right thing. So we can imagine a world in which everyone freely chooses every time to do the right thing, and, since God is all-powerful, He must be able to create it.

But since God is also all-good, the objector continues, He would, of course, prefer such a world to any world infected with evil. If God had the choice between creating a flawless world and a world with evil in it like this one, He would surely choose the flawless world. Otherwise, He would Himself be evil to prefer that His creatures experience pain and suffering when He could have given them happiness and prosperity.

The eighteenth-century Scottish skeptic David Hume summarized the logical problem of evil nicely when he asked concerning God, "Is He willing to prevent evil, but not able? Then He is impotent. Is He able, but not willing? Then He is malevolent. Is He both able and willing? Whence then is evil?"[4]

But the fallacy with this line of argument is that the two assumptions made by the atheist objector are not necessarily true. In the first place, it is not necessarily true that an all-powerful God can create just

[4] David Hume, *Dialogues Concerning Natural Religion,* edited with an introduction by Norman Kemp Smith (Indianapolis: Bobbs-Merrill, 1980), part 10, 198.

any possible world. God's being all-powerful does not mean that He can do logical impossibilities, such as make a round square, or make someone freely choose to do something. If you cause a person to make a specific choice, then the choice is no longer free. Thus, if God grants people genuine freedom to choose as they like, then it is impossible for Him to determine what their choices will be. All He can do is create the circumstances in which a person is able to make a free choice and then stand back and let him make that choice. Now what that means is that there may be worlds that are possible in and of themselves, but that God is incapable of creating. Suppose, for example, that in every world where God created free creatures those creatures would freely choose to do evil. In such a case, it is the creatures themselves who bring about the evil, and God can do nothing to prevent their doing so unless He removes their free will. Thus it is possible that every world God could create containing free creatures would be a world with sin and evil.

Moreover, as for natural evils, those could be the result of demonic activity in the world. Demons have freedom just as do human beings, and it is possible that God could not preclude natural evil without removing the free will of demonic creatures. Now you might be thinking that such a resolution to the problem of natural evil is ridiculous and even frivolous, but then you would be confusing the *logical* problem of evil with the *probabilistic* problem of evil. Admittedly, ascribing all evil to demonic beings is improbable, but that is strictly irrelevant here. All we are trying to show now is that such an explanation is possible and that, as a consequence, the atheist's argument that God and evil are logically incompatible fails.

So the first assumption made by the atheist objector, namely, that an all-powerful God can create any world that He chooses, is just not necessarily true. Therefore, the objector's argument on this ground alone is invalid.

But what about the second assumption, that if God is all-good, then He would prefer a world without evil over a world with evil? Again, such an assumption is not necessarily true. The fact is that in many cases we allow pain and suffering to occur in a person's life in

order to bring about some greater good or because we have some sufficient reason for allowing it. Every parent knows this fact. There
comes a point at which a parent can no longer protect his child from
every scrape, bruise, or mishap; and there are other times when discipline must be inflicted on the child in order to teach him to become
a mature, responsible adult. Similarly, God may permit suffering in
our lives to build us or to test us, or to build and test others, or to
achieve some other overriding end.

Sometimes this process can be very painful, as C. S. Lewis discovered upon the death of his wife. Comparing God to a Cosmic
Surgeon rather than to a Cosmic Sadist, Lewis mused,

> The terrible thing is that a perfectly good God is . . . hardly less
> formidable than a Cosmic Sadist. The more we believe that God
> hurts only to heal, the less we can believe that there is any use in
> begging for tenderness. A cruel man might be bribed—might grow
> tired of his vile sport—might have a temporary fit of mercy, as alco-
> holics have fits of sobriety. But suppose that what you are up
> against is a surgeon whose intentions are wholly good. The kinder
> and more conscientious he is, the more inexorably he will go on
> cutting. If he yielded to your entreaties, if he stopped before the
> operation was complete, all the pain up to that point would have
> been useless.
>
> What do people mean when they say, "I am not afraid of God
> because I know He is good"? Have they never even been to a dentist?[5]

Thus, even though God is all-good, He might well have sufficient
reasons for permitting pain and suffering in the world. Consequently,
the second assumption of our atheist objector, that an all-good God
would prefer a world with no evil over a world with evil, is not necessarily true.

The bottom line is that the logical version of the problem of evil
does not stand up to scrutiny. No one has been able to formulate a
valid argument to prove that God and evil are inconsistent.

---

[5] C. S. Lewis, *A Grief Observed* (London: Faber & Faber, 1985), 55-56.

But those who propound the logical problem of evil can regroup and return for a second wave of attack. They can admit that there is no inconsistency between God and evil in general but still argue that the existence of God is inconsistent with the *quantity* and *quality* of evil in the world. In other words, though abstractly speaking there is no inconsistency between God and evil, there is an inconsistency between God and the amount and kinds of evil that actually exist. For example, even if God's existence is compatible with, say, the fact that innocent persons are sometimes murdered, it is not compatible with the fact that so *many* people are killed and that they are killed in such torturous, gruesome ways. An all-good and powerful God would not permit such things to happen.

But the crucial assumption behind this reasoning is that *God cannot have morally sufficient reasons for permitting the amount and kinds of evil that exist.* The failing in this assumption is that it is just not clear that the assumption is necessarily true. Consider first the amount of evil in the world. As terrible a place as the world is, there is still on balance a great deal more good in the world than evil. Otherwise everyone would commit suicide. But people generally agree that despite its ills life is worth living, and when things are going bad, people characteristically look to the future in hope that things will get better.

Now it's possible, given human freedom, that in any other world God could have created, the balance between good and evil would have been even worse than in this one. That is to say, any world containing less *evil* might also have contained less *good.* Maybe the world we presently have has in it the most good God could get for the least amount of evil. Now you might say that seems pretty unlikely. But then you would be confusing once again the *logical* problem of evil with the *probabilistic* problem of evil. To refute the logical version of the problem of evil, the Christian does not have to suggest a *plausible* or *likely* solution—all he has to do is suggest a *possible* one. All he needs to do is show that God and the amount of evil in the world are both *possible*—and that he seems to have done.

Now consider the *kinds* of evil in the world. The Christian believes that God has overriding reasons for permitting the world's most terrible atrocities to occur. For example, it may be that God places such a premium on human freedom that He is willing to permit atrocities to occur rather than to remove the free will of those who commit them. (Perhaps God will punish the wrongdoers in the afterlife and comfort those who were victimized, but that is beside the point at this stage of the argument.) Similarly, if we adopt the hypothesis that natural evils are the result of the free activity of demons, then the same point about free will applies there, too. Now it still might be objected that God could have created a world of free creatures in which they committed fewer atrocities. But then the same argument applies as before: though it is possible that in such a world there would be less *evil,* there might also have been less *good.*

The point is, if the objector aims to show that it is logically impossible for God and the evil in the world to both exist, then he has to prove that God cannot have morally sufficient reasons for permitting the amount and kinds of evil that exist. And he hasn't given us any proof for that assumption.

We can go even further than this. Not only has the objector failed to prove that God and evil are inconsistent, but we can, on the contrary, prove that they are consistent. In order to do that, all we have to do is provide some possible explanation of the evil in the world that is compatible with God's existence. And the following is such an explanation:

> God could not have created a world that had so much good as the actual world but had less evil, both in terms of quantity and quality; and, moreover, God has morally sufficient reasons for the evil that exists.

So long as this explanation is even possible, it proves that God and the evil in the world are logically compatible.

So, to sum up our discussion of the logical problem of evil, we have seen that there is no necessary incompatibility between the presence of an all-good, all-powerful God and the presence of evil in the world. And I'm extremely pleased to report to you that after centuries of discussion, contemporary philosophy has come to recognize this fact. It is now widely admitted that the logical problem of evil has been solved. (Praise the Lord for Christian philosophers like Alvin Plantinga to whom this result is due!)[6]

But before we breathe too easily, we have to confront the probabilistic problem of evil. This we shall do in the next chapter.

---

[6] This chapter is a popularization of the Free Will Defense laid out by Plantinga in *The Nature of Necessity* (Oxford: Clarendon, 1974), 164-195; see further, Alvin Plantinga, "Self-Profile," in James Tomberlin and Peter Van Inwagen, eds., *Alvin Plantinga,* Profiles, vol. 5. (Dordrecht, Holland: D. Reidel, 1985), 36-55.

5

SUFFERING AND EVIL (II)

When we consider the probabilistic problem of evil, things are not so easy. For even though the explanation of evil I gave in the last chapter is possible, still it seems wildly improbable. Explaining all natural evil as the result of demons, for example, seems ridiculous. Does anyone really believe that earthquakes are the result of demons moving tectonic plates about or that when he stubs his toe the devil made him do it? And couldn't God reduce the evil in the world without reducing the good? To recall the tragedy in Mexico City, what impairment of the good of the world would have resulted if the child had simply died in the collapse of the building instead of lingering eleven days in agony? The world is filled with so many seemingly pointless and unnecessary evils that it seems doubtful that God could have any sort of morally sufficient reason for permitting them. Accordingly, it might be argued that given the evil in the world, it is improbable, even if not impossible, that God exists.

Now this is a much more powerful argument than the purely logical problem of evil. Since its conclusion is more modest ("It is improbable that God exists"), it is much easier to prove. What shall we say about this argument? Is it improbable that God exists?

Well, to begin with, let's note a very important—indeed, crucial—difference between a probability argument like this one and a purely logical argument like the one we had before. In the case of a purely logical argument, all you have to consider is the argument itself. If the logical problem of evil is a sound argument, then God cannot exist, period, no questions asked. But with a probability argument, we have to ask: probable with respect to what? To give an illustration: suppose Joe is a college student. Suppose, further, that 95 percent of college students drink beer. With respect to that information, it makes it highly probable that Joe drinks beer. But suppose we find out that Joe is a Wheaton College student and that 95 percent of Wheaton students do not drink beer. Suddenly the probability of Joe's being a beer drinker has changed dramatically! The point is that probabilities are relative to what background information is considered.

Now apply this principle to the probabilistic problem of evil. It claims to prove that God's existence is improbable. But with respect to what? With respect to the evil in the world? If that's all you consider, then I should hardly be surprised that God's existence would appear improbable with respect to that. Indeed, I should consider it to be a major philosophical achievement if Christians could demonstrate that relative to the evil in the world alone, God's existence is not improbable. But the Christian needn't be committed to such an arduous task. He will insist that we consider, not just the evil in the world, but all the evidence relevant to God's existence, including the ontological argument for a maximally great being, the cosmological argument for a Creator of the universe, the teleological argument for an intelligent Designer of the cosmos, the noölogical argument for an ultimate Mind, the axiological argument for an ultimate, personally embodied Good, as well as evidence concerning the person of Christ, the historicity of the resurrection, the existence of miracles, plus existential and religious experience.[1] When we take into account the full scope of the evidence, the existence of God becomes quite probable. Hence, a Christian could actually admit that the problem of evil, taken in isolation, does make God's existence improbable. But he will

---

[1] For a discussion of such arguments see William Lane Craig, ed., *Philosophy of Religion: A Reader and Guide* (Edinburgh: Edinburgh University Press, 2002; New Brunswick, N.J.: Rutgers University Press, 2002).

insist that when the total scope of the evidence is considered, then the scales are at least even or tip in favor of Christianity. Indeed, if he includes the self-authenticating witness of the Holy Spirit as part of his total warrant, then he can rightly assert that he knows that God exists, even if he has no solution at all to the problem of evil.

In fact, the Christian might insist that insofar as the probabilistic problem of evil is taken to be an internal problem, there is nothing whatsoever objectionable or irrational about believing statements which are improbable with respect to each other, so long as one knows them both to be true. For example, relative to what we know about human reproductive biology, your own personal existence is astronomically improbable. Yet there is nothing irrational about believing both the facts of human reproductive biology and that you exist. Similarly, if one is warranted in believing that God exists, then there is no problem in the fact that this belief is improbable relative to the evil in the world.

So even though the probabilistic problem of evil is a lot easier to support than the logical problem of evil, it is, even when successful, a whole lot less decisive.

But is it in fact successful? Given the existence of the evil in the world, is it improbable that God exists? This is far from clear. It all depends on how probable it is that God has morally sufficient reasons for permitting the evil that occurs.

What makes the probability here so difficult to assess is that we are just so ignorant of God's designs. We are simply not in a position to know why God permits various evils to occur. Certainly many evils seem pointless and gratuitous to us—but how can we be sure they really are? Perhaps they fit into a wider picture. According to the biblical scheme of things, God is directing human history toward His previsioned ends. Now can you possibly imagine the complexity of planning and directing a world of free creatures toward some end without violating their freedom? Think of the innumerable, incalculable contingencies involved in arriving at a single historical event, say, the Allied victory at D-Day! It may well be that in order to arrive at some end, God must permit sinful actions and natural evils to enter into the picture.

Take the Holocaust, for example. Few more horrific events in history can be imagined. Probably millions of people lost their faith in God through this cataclysm. But suppose that the only way God could get the nations of the world to freely establish the modern state of Israel was by allowing the Holocaust, an event so ghastly, so unparalleled in history, directed at a single persecuted people, that the world in shame and sympathy took the remarkable step of restoring the Jews to their ancient homeland. I want to say emphatically that this does not mean the Holocaust was, after all, good. That would be absurd. It was a hideous illustration of human depravity, sin piled upon sin, contrary to God's perfect will. But perhaps God had a morally sufficient reason to permit it, namely, the establishment of the nation of Israel. A church father once said of the early Christian martyrs that the blood of the martyrs was the seed of the church. Perhaps future generations of Israelis will say with gratitude the same thing of those who died in the Holocaust. And who knows what future plans God has in store for the nation of Israel? Perhaps Israel will play so significant a role in world events that all nations will see that God had a morally sufficient reason for permitting the Holocaust.

The same point might be made on an individual level. We just don't know how the sufferings we endure might be used of God in our lives or, if not in ours, in the lives of those around us. Yes, they often look pointless, but we are simply not in a position to judge. Two illustrations, one from science and the other from popular culture: In the recently developing field of Chaos Theory, scientists have discovered that certain macroscopic systems, for example, weather systems or insect populations, are extraordinarily sensitive to the tiniest perturbations. A butterfly fluttering on a branch in West Africa may set in motion forces which would eventually issue in a hurricane over the Atlantic Ocean. Yet it is impossible in principle for anyone observing that butterfly palpitating on a branch to predict such an outcome. The second illustration is from the movie *Sliding Doors*. In this film a young woman's life is dramatically affected by whether or not she manages to catch a subway train before the doors slide shut. The film shows that in one case her subsequent life is prosperous and wildly successful, whereas in the other case it is filled with suffering and dis-appointment. All because of the seemingly trivial incident of catch-ing/missing a subway train! But that's not all. At the film's end we discover to our surprise that the course of her life which is filled with hardship actually turns out to be the better life, while the seemingly happy life ends prematurely in tragedy.

The point I'm trying to make is that assessments of probability with regard to evil can be very difficult and even impossible. Certainly many evils seem pointless and unnecessary to us—but we are simply not in a position to judge. The brutal murder of an innocent man or a child's dying of leukemia could send a ripple effect through history so that God's morally sufficient reason for permitting it might not emerge until centuries later or perhaps in another country. To say this is not to appeal to mystery, but rather to point to the inherent cogni-tive limitations that frustrate attempts to say that it is improbable that God has a morally sufficient reason for permitting some particular evil. Events which appear disastrous in the short term may redound to the greatest good, while some short-term boon may issue in untold misery. Once we contemplate God's providence over the whole of history, then it becomes evident how hopeless it is for limited observers to speculate on the probability of God's having morally suf-ficient reasons for the evils that we see. We are simply not in a good position to assess such probabilities with any confidence.

But much more can be said concerning the probabilistic problem of evil. The atheist maintains that if God exists, then it is improbable that the world would contain the evil it does. Now what the Christian can do in response to such an assertion is to offer various hypotheses that would tend to raise the probability of evil given God's existence. The Christian can show that if God exists and these hypotheses are true, then it is not so surprising that evil exists. Therefore, the exis-tence of evil doesn't render God's existence improbable.[2]

---

[2] I am indebted for the following to Robert Merrihew Adams, "Plantinga on the Problem of Evil," in James Tomberlin and Peter Van Inwagen, eds., *Alvin Plantinga,* Profiles, vol. 5. (Dordrecht, Holland: D. Reidel, 1985), 225-255; and to Marilyn McCord Adams, "Problem of Evil: More Advice to Christian Philosophers," *Faith and Philosophy* 5 (1988): 121-143.

What are some of those hypotheses? They are doctrines that emerge from the Christian concept of God. It turns out that answering the probabilistic problem of evil is easier from the Christian perspective than from the perspective of belief in the mere existence of God. Since the problem is being presented as an internal problem for the Christian, there is nothing illicit about the Christian's availing himself of all the resources of his worldview in answering the objection. I shall mention four Christian doctrines in this connection:

First, the chief purpose of life is not happiness, but the knowledge of God. One reason that the problem of evil seems so intractable is that people tend naturally to assume that if God exists, then His purpose for human life is happiness in this life. God's role is to provide a comfortable environment for His human pets. But on the Christian view, this is false. We are not God's pets, and the goal of human life is not happiness *per se,* but the knowledge of God—which in the end will bring true and everlasting human fulfillment. Many evils occur in life which may be utterly pointless with respect to the goal of producing human happiness; but they may not be pointless with respect to producing a deeper knowledge of God. Dostoyevsky, who stated the problem of evil so forcefully, saw this point and sought to answer the problem in his novels through the portrayal of characters who through suffering increase in godliness and holiness. Innocent human suffering provides an occasion for deeper dependency and trust in God, on the part of either the sufferer or of those around him. Of course, whether God's purpose is achieved through our suffering will depend on our response. Do we respond with anger and bitterness toward God, or do we turn to Him in faith for strength to endure?

Because God's ultimate goal for humanity is our knowledge of Him—which alone can bring eternal happiness—history cannot be seen in its true perspective apart from considerations pertinent to the kingdom of God. The British divine Martyn Lloyd-Jones has written,

The key to the history of the world is the kingdom of God. . . . From the very beginning, . . . God has been at work establishing a new kingdom in the world. It is His own kingdom, and He is calling people out of the world into that kingdom: and everything that happens in the world has relevance to it. . . . Other events are of importance as they have a bearing upon that event. The problems of today are to be understood only in its light. . . .

Let us not therefore be stumbled when we see surprising things happening in the world. Rather let us ask, "What is the relevance of this event to the kingdom of God?" Or, if strange things are happening to you personally, don't complain but say, "What is God teaching me through this?" . . . We need not become bewildered and doubt the love or the justice of God. . . . We should . . . judge every event in the light of God's great, eternal and glorious purpose.[3]

It may well be the case that natural and moral evils are part of the means God uses to draw people into His kingdom. This was brought home to me several years ago as I worked through Patrick Johnstone's *Operation World*. It is precisely in countries that have endured severe hardship that evangelical Christianity is growing at its greatest rates, while growth curves in the indulgent West are nearly flat. Consider, for example, the following reports[4]:

China: It is estimated that 20 million Chinese lost their lives during [Mao's Cultural Revolution]. . . . Christians . . . stood firm in what was probably the most widespread and harsh persecution the Church has ever experienced. The persecution purified and indigenized the Church. . . . The growth of the Church in China since 1977 has no parallels in history. Researchers estimated [that there were] 30-75 million Christians [by 1990]. . . . Mao Zedong unwittingly became the greatest evangelist in history.

El-Salvador: The 12-year civil war, earthquakes, and the collapse of the price of coffee, the nation's main export, impoverished the nation. . . . Over 80% live in dire poverty. . . . An astonishing spiri-

3 David Martyn Lloyd-Jones, *From Fear to Faith* (London: Intervarsity Press, 1953), 23-24.
4 Patrick Johnstone, *Operation World* (Grand Rapids, Mich.: Zondervan, 1993), 163-164, 207-208, 214.

tual harvest has been gathered from all strata of society in the midst of the hate and bitterness of war. In 1960, evangelicals were 2.3% of the population, but today are around 20%.

Ethiopia: Ethiopia is in a state of shock. Her population struggles with the trauma of millions of deaths through repression, famine and war. . . . Two great waves of violent persecution . . . refined and purified the Church, but there were many martyrs. . . . There have been . . . millions coming to Christ. Protestants were fewer than . . . 0.8% of the population . . . in 1960, but by 1990 this may have become . . . 13% of the population.

Examples such as these could be multiplied. The history of mankind has been a history of suffering and war. Yet it has also been a history of the advance of the kingdom of God. A chart released in 1990 by the U.S. Center for World Mission documented the amazing growth in evangelical Christianity over the centuries. The researchers who compiled the data estimated that, in A.D. 100, for every evangelical believer in the world there were 360 non-Christians. By the year 1000 there were 220 non-Christians for every evangelical believer in the world. By 1900 that ratio had shrunk to 27 non-Christians per evangelical believer. And by 1989, for every evangelical believer in the world there were only 7 non-Christians.[5]

According to Johnstone, "We are living in the time of the largest ingathering of people into the Kingdom of God that the world has ever seen."[6] It is not at all improbable that this astonishing growth in God's kingdom is due in part to the presence of natural and moral evils in the world.

Second, mankind is in a state of rebellion against God and His purpose. Rather than submit to and worship God, people rebel against God and go their own way and so find themselves alienated from God, morally guilty before Him, groping in spiritual darkness, and pursuing false gods of their own making. The terrible human evils in the

[5] Ralph D. Winter, *Mission Frontiers,* November 1990, 18.
[6] Johnstone, *Operation World,* 25.

world are testimony to man's depravity in his state of spiritual alien-ation from God. Moreover, there is a realm of beings higher than man also in rebellion against God, demonic creatures, incredibly evil, in whose power the creation lies (1 John 5:19) and who seek to destroy God's work and thwart His purposes. The Christian is thus not sur-prised at the moral evil in the world; on the contrary, he *expects* it. The Scriptures indicate that God has given mankind up to the sin it has freely chosen; He does not interfere to stop it but lets human depravity run its course (Rom. 1:24, 26, 28). This only serves to heighten mankind's moral responsibility before God, as well as our wickedness and our need of forgiveness and moral cleansing.

Third, God's purpose is not restricted to this life but spills over beyond the grave into eternal life. According to Christianity, this life is but the cramped and narrow foyer opening up into the great hall of God's eternity. God promises eternal life to all those who place their trust in Christ as Savior and Lord. When God asks His children to bear horrible suffering in this life, it is only with the prospect of a heavenly joy and recompense that is beyond all comprehension. Moreover, there is an eternal life following this one that awaits those who have trusted God in faith and obedience in this life.

The apostle Paul, for example, for the sake of the gospel underwent suffering that was, when you reflect on it, unbelievable. It would be a devastating experience, not only physically excruciating but possibly even permanently crippling emotionally, to be whipped for a crime you didn't commit. But Paul was whipped five different times just for preaching the gospel, each time receiving twenty-six lashes to the back and thirteen to his breast with a triple-thonged whip. Not only that, but three times more he was stripped and beaten by Roman authori-ties with wooden rods. On one occasion in the city of Lystra he was surrounded by a mob, who stoned him and dragged his body out of the city, leaving him for dead. Can you imagine what it must feel like to be stoned? You could probably only pray that someone would knock you out quickly with a rock to the head; but probably you wouldn't be so lucky. It would be a horrible way to die. Paul's body must have been a mass of scars, wounds inflicted for no better reason than his being a Christian. No wonder he could say indignantly of those who denied his apostleship, "Finally, let no one cause me trouble, for I bear on my body the marks of Jesus" (Gal. 6:17).

People who have been imprisoned, even for a few months, have also testified what a life-shattering experience this sort of confinement can be. But Paul was frequently imprisoned for his faith for lengthy intervals in Roman jails, under what by modern standards could only be described as unspeakable conditions: unheated, unsanitary, bound hand and foot with chains. He called himself "a prisoner for Jesus Christ."

On top of all this, Paul suffered from natural disasters, too. For example, he apparently suffered from a debilitating illness, which some have speculated to have been epilepsy or some sort of eye disease. Furthermore, he was involved in three separate shipwrecks on the Mediterranean Sea. Can you imagine what it would be like to be involved in even one wreck at sea? But three times? And in one of those, Paul was adrift at sea for a night and a day before being saved. Can you imagine the terror of being adrift at sea in the night, desperately clutching some piece of wreckage, trying to fight off exhaustion, hour after hour, in constant peril of drowning? Moreover, in his travels throughout the Roman Empire preaching the gospel, Paul was constantly in danger from both human enemies and natural disasters. There were dangerous river crossings, and robbers were a threat while on the road. At any time, whether in the cities where he preached, or in the countryside, or at sea while he traveled, he could be set upon by enemies who sought his life. Whether those enemies were Jews, Gentiles, or false Christians, each of them had their particular reasons to get rid of Paul. He worked long, hard hours, often going without sleep, frequently without food, and without adequate protection from exposure to the elements. And psychologically, he bore the constant burden of anxiety for the fledgling Christian churches he had founded, which seemed to be in constant danger of being torn apart by heresies. In the end, in Rome, Paul made the ultimate sacrifice and was executed for his faith.

In sum, Paul's life as an apostle was a life of incredible hardship and suffering, one which he described as punctuated by "afflictions, hardships, calamities, beatings, imprisonments, tumults, labors, watching, hunger" (2 Cor. 6:4-5, RSV); the apostles were ignominious, misunderstood, and slandered, and possessed virtually nothing materially in this world. And yet Paul bore his sufferings without bitterness. Why? *Because it was worth it.* He understood that this life is but the antechamber to eternity, and he longed to go and be with Christ. He wrote,

> So we do not lose heart. Though our outer nature is wasting away, our inner nature is being renewed every day. For this slight momentary affliction is preparing for us an eternal weight of glory beyond all comparison, because we look not to the things that are seen but to the things that are unseen; for the things that are seen are transient, but the things that are unseen are eternal (2 Cor. 4:16-18, RSV).

Can you believe it? After what this man suffered, he calls it a "slight, momentary affliction"! You see, Paul lived this life in the perspective of eternity. He understood that the length of this life, being finite, is literally infinitesimal in comparison with the eternal life we shall spend with God. The longer we spend in eternity, the more the sufferings of this life will shrink toward an infinitesimal moment. It may well be that there are evils in the world that serve no earthly good at all, that are entirely gratuitous from a human point of view, but which God permits simply that He might overwhelmingly reward in the afterlife those who undergo such evils with faith and confidence in God.

One reason the problem of evil seems so intractable to us today is because we no longer live in this perspective. To borrow Paul's phrase, we look to the things that are seen, not to the things that are unseen. As the old beer commercial put it, "You only go around once in life, so grab for all the gusto you can get." With such a shallow, selfish view of life, it is no wonder we can't understand how God could permit us to suffer: it doesn't contribute to our gusto! Even as Christians, we absorb this worldly attitude. The pressures and affairs of this life seem so real and so urgent that we forget to lift up our eyes beyond the horizons of our own life to the eternal life that waits for us beyond.

But when we keep in mind that life does not end at the grave and that in heaven God "will wipe away every tear from [our] eyes; there shall be no more death, nor sorrow, nor crying. There shall be no more pain" (Rev. 21:4, NKJV), but only the fullness of divine joy and glory, then the problem of evil does not seem so severe. As Tolstoy once put it (in his short story by that name), "God sees the truth, but waits." In the end, divine rewards and punishments will do more than enough to make up for what we have suffered here.

Fourth, the knowledge of God is an incommensurable good. When I first became a Christian, it struck me that in order to obtain eternal life in heaven, it would be worth it if God asked us to undergo an earthly life of the most extreme asceticism, suffering, and self-denial, but that God in His graciousness doesn't even ask us to do that; instead, He fills our lives with peace, joy, love, meaning, and purpose. But no matter what He asked us to endure, it would be worth it to gain heaven. The passage cited above from Paul also serves to make this point. He imagines, as it were, a scale, in which all the sufferings and rottenness of this life are placed on the one side, while on the other side is placed the glory that God will give to His children in heaven. And the weight of glory is so great that it is literally beyond comparison with the sufferings we endure. That's why Paul called the sufferings of this life a "slight, momentary affliction": he wasn't being insensitive to the plight of those who suffer horribly in this life—on the contrary, he was one of them—but he saw that those sufferings were simply overwhelmed by the ocean of joy and glory that God will give to those who trust Him. For to know God, the locus of infinite goodness and love, is an incomparable good, the fulfillment of human existence. The sufferings of this life cannot even be compared to it. Thus, the person who knows God, no matter what he suffers, no matter how awful his pain, can still truly say, "God is good to me!" simply by virtue of the fact that he knows God, an incommensurable good.

These four Christian doctrines increase the probability of the coexistence of God and the evils in the world. They thereby serve to decrease any improbability that these evils might seem to cast upon the existence of God.

So it seems that the probabilistic problem of evil is far from unanswerable. Even if God's existence is improbable relative to the evil in the world alone, that does not make God's existence improbable, for balancing off the negative evidence from evil is the positive evidence for God's existence. Moreover, it is extremely difficult to establish from the evil in the world that God's existence is improbable, for God could have morally sufficient reasons for permitting such evil. We do not find ourselves in a good position to judge with any confidence that this is improbable. Finally, we can render the coexistence of God and evil more probable by adopting certain hypotheses inherent in the Christian worldview, for example, that the purpose of life is the knowledge of God, that mankind is in a state of rebellion against God and His purpose, that God's purpose extends beyond the grave to eternal life, and that the knowledge of God is an incommensurable good. Taken together, these considerations make it not improbable that God and the evil in the world should both exist. Thus, the probabilistic version of the internal problem of evil seems no more decisive than the logical version.

But if the problem of evil fails as an internal problem for Christianity, does it present an insuperable *external problem?* The versions of the problem I have discussed so far tried to show that two beliefs held by Christians, namely that God exists and that the world contains the evils we observe, are either inconsistent or improbable with respect to each other. Most atheists have now abandoned the internal problem in their attacks upon Christianity. Instead they claim that the apparently pointless and unnecessary evils in the world—usually referred to as *gratuitous* evil—constitute *evidence* against God's existence. That is to say, they argue that the two statements "An all-powerful, all-good God exists" and "Gratuitous evil exists" are incompatible with each other. What makes this an external problem is that the Christian is not committed to admitting the truth of the statement "Gratuitous evil exists." The Christian is committed to the truth that "Evil exists," but not that "Gratuitous evil exists." The atheist objector is therefore arguing that the presence of gratuitous evil in the world disproves the existence of God.

The key question here will be whether we have good evidence to think that gratuitous evil exists. The Christian will readily admit that much of the evil we observe in the world appears to be pointless and unnecessary and, hence, gratuitous. But he will challenge the objector's inference from the appearance of gratuitous evil to the reality of gratuitous evil. Here much of what I've already said about the probabilistic internal problem of evil will be relevant. For example, the objector must assume that if we cannot discern God's morally sufficient reason for allowing certain evils to occur, then it is probable that there is no such reason. But we've seen how uncertain and tenuous such probability judgments on our part are. Our failure to discern the morally justifying reason for the occurrence of various evils gives very little ground for thinking that God—especially an all-knowing God who sees the end of history from the beginning and providentially orders the world—could not have morally sufficient reasons for permitting the evils we observe in the world. Moreover, my point about the necessity of considering the full scope of the evidence is also relevant. For when we ask whether the evil we observe in the world really is gratuitous, the most important question we must consider is, ironically, whether God exists. For if the statements "An all-powerful, all-good God exists" and "Gratuitous evil exists" are incompatible, as the atheist claims, then it follows logically that if God exists, then gratuitous evil does not exist, or in other words that the evil in the world only *appears* to be gratuitous but in fact is not. As Daniel Howard-Snyder points out, the problem of evil is thus a problem only for the person who finds all its premises and inferences compelling and who has lousy grounds for believing in God; but if one has more compelling grounds for believing in God, then the problem of evil "is not a problem."[7]

It should also be noted that the atheist's claim that the statements

[7] Daniel Howard-Snyder, "Introduction," in Daniel Howard-Snyder, ed., *The Evidential Argument from Evil* (Bloomington: Indiana University Press, 1996), p xi.

"An all-powerful, all-good God exists" and "Gratuitous evil exists" are incompatible is not itself obviously true. Some Christian philosophers have suggested that while God could eliminate this or that specific evil without decreasing the goodness of the world, nevertheless there must exist a certain amount of gratuitous evil in the world if the goodness of the world is not to be impaired. Thus the existence of gratuitous evil would not disprove the existence of God. In fact it is possible that only in a world in which gratuitous natural and moral evils exist the optimal number of persons would freely come to accept the offer of salvation and find the knowledge of God. The atheist might protest that in that case the evils would not really be gratuitous after all: they would serve the greater good of securing people's eternal salvation. So the Christian must deny that gratuitous evil exists, despite the evidence to the contrary. But if one allows a greater good like salvation to count against the apparent pointlessness of some evil, then that makes it all the more difficult for the atheist to prove that truly gratuitous evil exists, for how could he possibly surmise what in God's providential plan for history does or does not contribute to the ultimate salvation of the greatest number of people?

So we may never know why God permits any particular evil in our lives. But why should we know? Remember the York signal box mistake? Since we're not in the control tower, we shouldn't expect to be able to know why every evil is permitted by God or how it fits into His plan. But more than that: if the Christian story is true, then we don't need to know either. We are simply called upon to trust in God and His goodness no matter what the circumstances. This is not blind faith, for there are good reasons to believe in God's existence, and we have the self-authenticating witness of His Spirit as well. We are not called upon to figure out why God has permitted us to suffer some evil; we are called upon to trust Him.

This is, I think, the true message of the book of Job. For many years I never really liked the book of Job because it doesn't ever explain why God permits evil in the world. God's answer to Job out of the whirlwind doesn't explain anything. But I think I've come to see the wisdom of the book of Job. God is saying, "You don't need to know why I permit terrible suffering and evil in the world. That's My business. What you need to learn is to trust Me in spite of everything." That's what Job did. "Though he slay me, yet I will hope in him" (Job 13:15a). And God rewarded him many times over. It may well be that there are evils in the world that serve no earthly good at all, that are entirely gratuitous from a human point of view, but which God permits simply that He might overwhelmingly reward in the after-life those who undergo such evils in faith and confidence in Him. To reiterate a point made earlier, it may well be the case that God is not so much concerned with *what* you go through as with your *attitude* while you go through it.

So it seems to me that from the Christian point of view the exis-tence of the moral evil in the world becomes understandable. The purpose of human life is not happiness as such, but the knowledge of God. In order to bring people to salvation or into a deeper relation-ship with Him, God may permit great suffering in our lives. There may be no purpose for this suffering in earthly terms at all, but it may be a summons to trust in God with the prospect of a reward in heaven that is literally incomparable to the suffering, both in its greatness and its duration.

But what about natural evil? Again, elements in the Christian story can help to make it more understandable. To begin with, it is important to see how inextricably intertwined natural evil is with human, moral evil. Imagine that there were no moral evil in the world, that everybody lived in accordance with the teachings of Jesus—what a wonderful world that would be! If there were a drought in Ethiopia, the world would rush to the aid of the people there to prevent famine. The wealth of the world would be largely redistributed, instead of being hoarded in the materialistic Western nations. As a result, disease would greatly diminish, medical care would be more readily available, and people would live in decent housing instead of shacks or shoddily constructed tenement houses that are demolished in natural catastrophes. Think of the mercy and the love that would be shown to those who suffer! Of course, terri-ble natural evils would remain and accidents would still occur, but if there were no moral evil, many natural evils would disappear or be greatly reduced.

Second, a world containing gratuitous natural evils may be necessary for people to come to a knowledge of God. God's overriding aim is for people to come to the knowledge of Himself in a free, uncoerced way. Perhaps it is just a fact that only in a world containing pointless natural suffering would people turn to God. Who knows? It may be that God has created a world containing natural evils that don't contribute to any higher good in this life but which serve as the context in which He knew people would freely believe and trust in Him.

Finally, God may have simply created a world operating physically according to certain natural laws and then, for the most part, sat back and let nature run its course. Of course, He may intervene sometimes to do a miracle, but that is the exception rather than the rule. It is not wrong of Him to permit natural evils, for in the afterlife He rewards with an incommensurable good those who endure in faith those natural afflictions. Though He may not intervene physically in most cases to prevent suffering, that does not mean He is uninvolved, for by His Spirit He is ever there to strengthen and comfort the suffering.

But let's get specific and see how this reasoning would apply to the two incidents that so graphically portrayed to me the problem of evil: the Mexican boy who slowly died from the collapse of a building and the Colombian girl who drowned in the aftermath of the mudslide. In the first place, both incidents concerned natural evils intertwined with human moral sin. The whole of Latin America has been victimized by an unjust and uncaring upper class, which has, in its lust for power and wealth, exploited the masses, leaving them poor and underprivileged. The suffering of those two children is indirectly attributable to this corrupt and unchristian system, for if the societies in which the children lived were following Christian principles, their families would not have been forced to live in unsafe housing that was improperly located or so poorly built that it disintegrated under the stress of earthquake or rain. In a world free from sin, it's possible that neither of the tragedies would have taken place. Hence, man must shoulder some of the blame for those evils.

Why did God permit these children to suffer so? I don't know. Perhaps through the tragic death of this boy, God knew Mexican authorities would be shocked into requiring new construction standards for earthquake-proof buildings, thereby saving many future lives. Maybe He let it happen because the authorities should be so shocked. Maybe He permitted it so that some other person, facing death or illness in a hospital and seeing the reports on television, would be inspired by the boy's courage to face his own challenge with faith and bravery. Maybe God permitted the Colombian girl to slowly drown because He knew that only then would her family—or somebody else—turn to Him in faith and repentance. Or perhaps He knew that only through such a terrible incident would her family move away to a place where they, or even their descendants, might in turn come to be influenced or to influence someone else for Christ. We just don't know.

But maybe there wasn't any earthly reason why God permitted those catastrophes. Maybe they served no earthly good whatever. Perhaps the catastrophes were simply the unfortunate by-product of natural geological and meteorological laws and the children their unlucky victims. But God permitted this suffering in the lives of these children in order that they and their families might be driven into deeper dependence on Him. We don't know why God permitted this suffering, but this I do know: when that little girl and boy finally left this life and stepped into the next, Jesus enfolded them in His loving arms, wiped away their tears, and filled them with a glorious happiness beyond all expression, saying, "Well done, my child; enter into the joy of your Master." In that eternity of bliss, they will know a weight of glory beyond all comparison with what He asked them to suffer here. Therefore, the abused child described by Ivan Karamazov, who beat her breast with her little fist and cried out to "dear, kind God," did exactly the right thing, bless her soul, and shall not lose her reward, whereas Ivan in his rebellion against God found life too bitter to live.

Finally, there is one last point which I should like to make that seems to me to constitute a decisive refutation of the problem of evil, namely, the argument that evil proves that God exists. Yes, I believe that there is actually a proof from evil for the existence of God. This remarkable fact became clear to me as I was speaking on various university campuses in North America on "The Absurdity of Life Without God." In this lecture, I attempted to show that if God does not exist, then life is without ultimate meaning, value, or purpose. For apart from God, there is no standard of value; moral values simply become either expressions of personal taste or societal conventions adopted and instilled for the purpose of living together. My conclusion was a purely negative one: I never tried to show that objective values do exist, but only that without God they cannot exist.

But I found people repeatedly objecting that we can and do recognize that objective values do exist (for example, that racism or child abuse is really wrong and that love of one's neighbor is really good) and that we can know these values exist whether or not we know that God exists. Now clearly the objection the students raised didn't refute anything I had said. In fact, the Bible teaches that natural man, who has no knowledge of God, knows instinctively the moral law of God (Rom. 2:14-15).

But the experience impressed upon me that we all do sense that certain acts are really right or wrong, that objective values do exist. In essence what the students had done was add another premise to my argument that converted its purely negative conclusion into a positive one. For now the argument looks like this:

1. If God does not exist, then objective moral values do not exist.
2. Evil exists.
3. Therefore, objective moral values exist.
4. Therefore, God exists.

Step 1 was the point I was arguing and is agreed to by many Christians and atheists alike. Step 2 is the premise furnished by the problem of evil itself. Step 3 is the conclusion supplied by the university students, who saw that the moral evils in the world are objectively wrong. And step 4 is the logical conclusion of the argument: since objective moral values cannot exist without God and objective values do exist (as shown by the moral evil in the world), it follows that God exists. Therefore, evil actually proves that God exists.

If this argument is correct—and I think that it is—it constitutes a decisive refutation of the problem of evil. And notice that it does so without attempting to give any explanation at all for evil—we, like Job, may be totally ignorant of that—but it nonetheless shows that the very existence of evil in the world implies God's existence.

So in summary, I think we've seen that despite first appearances the intellectual problem of evil—whether in its internal or external forms—can be satisfactorily solved.

But, of course, when I say "solved" I mean "philosophically solved." All these mental machinations may be of little comfort to someone who is intensely suffering from some undeserved evil in life. I recall reading, for example, that when Joni Eareckson Tada suffered her paralyzing accident, there came a parade of people through her hospital room, each offering explanations as to why God had permitted this thing to happen to her. Though they were well-intentioned, to her these people took on the appearance of Job's comforters, and their rational explanations (a few of which were actually pretty good, I think!) came across as cold and uncaring. But this leads us to the second aspect of the problem I wanted to discuss: the emotional problem of evil.

You see, for many people, the problem of evil is not really an intellectual problem: it's an emotional problem. They're hurting inside and perhaps bitter against a God who would permit them or others to suffer so greatly. Never mind that there are philosophical solutions to the problem of evil—they don't care and simply reject a God who allows suffering such as we find in the world. It is interesting that in Dostoyevsky's *Brothers Karamazov* this is what the problem of evil finally comes down to. Ivan never refutes the Christian solution to the problem of evil. Instead, he just refuses to have anything to do with the Christian God. "I would rather remain with my unavenged suffering and unsatisfied indignation, *even if I am wrong,*" he declares.[8] His is simply an atheism of rejection.

What can we say to those who are laboring under the emotional problem of evil? In one sense, the most important thing may not be what you say at all. The most important thing is just to be there as a loving friend and sympathetic listener. But some people may need counsel, and we ourselves may need to deal with this problem when we suffer. Does the Christian faith also have something to say here?

It certainly does! For it tells us that God is not a distant Creator or impersonal ground of being, but a loving Father who shares our sufferings and hurts with us. Alvin Plantinga has written,

> As the Christian sees things, God does not stand idly by, cooly observing the suffering of His creatures. He enters into and shares our suffering. He endures the anguish of seeing his son, the second person of the Trinity, consigned to the bitterly cruel and shameful death of the cross. Some theologians claim that God cannot suffer. I believe they are wrong. God's capacity for suffering, I believe, is proportional to his greatness; it exceeds our capacity for suffering in the same measure as his capacity for knowledge exceeds ours. Christ was prepared to endure the agonies of hell itself; and God, the Lord of the universe, was prepared to endure the suffering consequent upon his son's humiliation and death. He was prepared to accept this suffering in order to overcome sin, and death, and the evils that afflict our world, and to confer on us a life more glorious than we can imagine. So we don't know why God permits evil; we do know, however, that He was prepared to suffer on our behalf, to accept suffering of which we can form no conception.[9]

You see, Jesus endured a suffering beyond all comprehension: He bore the punishment for the sins of the whole world. None of us can

---

[8] Fyodor Dostoevsky, *The Brothers Karamazov,* trans. Constance Garnett (Garden City, N.Y.: Doubleday, n.d.), 226.

[9] Alvin Plantinga, "Self-Profile," in *Alvin Plantinga,* 36.

comprehend that suffering. Though He was innocent, He voluntarily underwent the punishment for your sins and mine. And why? Because He loves you so much. How can you reject Him who gave up everything for you?

When we comprehend Christ's sacrifice and His love for us, this puts the problem of evil in an entirely different perspective. For now we see clearly that the true problem of evil is the problem of *our* evil. Filled with sin and morally guilty before God, the question we face is not how God can justify Himself to us, but how we can be justified before Him. If Christ has endured incomprehensible suffering for us to bring us to the saving knowledge of God, then surely we can endure the suffering that He asks us to bear in this life. Think of what He endured out of His love for you, and you will be able to more easily trust Him when you walk the path of pain yourself.

A former colleague of mine used to make it his habit to visit shut-ins in nursing homes in an attempt to bring a bit of cheer and love into their lives. One day he met a woman whom he could never forget:

> On this particular day I was walking in a hallway that I had not visited before, looking in vain for a few who were alive enough to receive a flower and a few words of encouragement. This hallway seemed to contain some of the worst cases, strapped onto carts or into wheelchairs and looking completely helpless.
>
> As I neared the end of this hallway, I saw an old woman strapped up in a wheelchair. Her face was an absolute horror. The empty stare and white pupils of her eyes told me that she was blind. The large hearing aid over one ear told me that she was almost deaf. One side of her face was being eaten by cancer. There was a discolored and running sore covering part of one cheek, and it had pushed her nose to one side, dropped one eye, and distorted her jaw so that what should have been the corner of her mouth was the bottom of her mouth. As a consequence, she drooled constantly. . . . I also learned later that this woman was eighty-nine years old and that she had been bedridden, blind, nearly deaf, and alone, for twenty-five years. This was Mabel.

I don't know why I spoke to her—she looked less likely to respond than most of the people I saw in that hallway. But I put a flower in her hand and said, "Here is a flower for you. Happy Mother's Day." She held the flower up to her face and tried to smell it, and then she spoke. And much to my surprise, her words, although somewhat garbled because of her deformity, were obviously produced by a clear mind. She said, "Thank you. It's lovely. But can I give it to someone else? I can't see it, you know, I'm blind."

I said, "Of course," and I pushed her in her chair back down the hallway to a place where I thought I could find some alert patients. I found one, and I stopped the chair. Mabel held out the flower and said, "Here, this is from Jesus."

That was when it began to dawn on me that this was not an ordinary human being. . . . . Mabel and I became friends over the next few weeks, and I went to see her once or twice a week for the next three years. . . . It was not many weeks before I turned from a sense that I was being helpful to a sense of wonder, and I would go to her with a pen and paper to write down the things she would say. . . .

During one hectic week of final exams I was frustrated because my mind seemed to be pulled in ten directions at once with all of the things that I had to think about. The question occurred to me, "What does Mabel have to think about—hour after hour, day after day, week after week, not even able to know if it's day or night?" So I went to her and asked, "Mabel, what do you think about when you lie here?"

And she said, "I think about my Jesus."

I sat there and thought for a moment about the difficulty, for me, of thinking about Jesus for even five minutes, and I asked, *"What* do you think about Jesus?" She replied slowly and deliberately as I wrote. And this is what she said:

> I think how good He's been to me. He's been awfully good
> to me in my life, you know. . . . I'm one of those kind who's
> mostly satisfied. . . . Lots of folks would think I'm kind of

old-fashioned. But I don't care. I'd rather have Jesus. He's all the world to me.

And then Mabel began to sing an old hymn:

Jesus is all the world to me,
My life, my joy, my all.
He is my strength from day to day,
Without him I would fall.
When I am sad, to him I go,
No other one can cheer me so.
When I am sad, He makes me glad.
He's my friend.

This is not fiction. Incredible as it may seem, a human being really lived like this. I know. I knew her. *How could she do it?* Seconds ticked and minutes crawled, and so did days and weeks and months and years of pain without human company and without an explanation of why it was all happening—and she lay there and sang hymns. *How could she do it?*

The answer, I think, is that Mabel had something that you and I don't have much of. She had power. Lying there in that bed, unable to move, unable to see, unable to hear, unable to talk to anyone, she had incredible power.[10]

Paradoxically, then, even though the problem of evil is the greatest objection to the existence of God, at the end of the day God is the only solution to the problem of evil. If God does not exist, then we are lost without hope in a life filled with gratuitous and unredeemed suffering. God is the final answer to the problem of evil, for He redeems us from evil and takes us into the everlasting joy of an incommensurable good: fellowship with Him.

[10] Thomas E. Schmidt, *Trying to Be Good: A Book of Doing for Thinking People* (Grand Rapids, Mich.: Zondervan, 1990), 180-183.

6

ABORTION

In recent U. S. presidential elections, the question of abortion has typically been one of the issues separating the candidates. In an effort to persuade people at the church we were attending at the time of an election to vote for the candidate who opposed abortion on demand, I put a newspaper ad on the bulletin board downstairs. It pictured a group of several little babies with the headline: "One out of every three babies conceived in the U.S. is aborted." This tragic statistic is accurate. But a week later as I passed through the hall, I noticed that someone had written these words across the ad: "Right-wing religious propaganda."

I was surprised at those words. Is that all there is to concern about 33 percent of conceptions ending in abortion: right-wing religious propaganda? Well, a lot of people certainly seem to think so. And that includes Christians. A friend recently showed me a letter written by a woman from our church who has since moved away. She gave six reasons for her supporting abortion:

1. Murder must have a malicious motive.
2. There are too many unwanted children in the world, and white couples don't like to adopt minority children.
3. The world's population is exploding too rapidly.
4. Most childless couples don't want to have children or adopt.
5. A woman's body is her own business; it should not be a political issue.

6. If people in underdeveloped nations are urged to have birth
control or abortion, the same policies should apply in developed nations.

What about these arguments? Do they suffice to justify abortion on
demand? Are people who oppose abortion little more than right-wing
religious propagandists?

It seems to me that amid the mass of arguments pro and con about
abortion, there are two central questions that will determine all the
others. How you answer these two fundamental questions will determine how you assess everything else. By focusing on these two central concerns, we can greatly clarify our thinking about the issue of
abortion. Here are the questions: (1) Do human beings possess
intrinsic moral value? and (2) Is the developing fetus a human being?

Let's think about that first question: *Do human beings have intrinsic
moral value?* Something has intrinsic value if it is an end in itself, rather
than a means to some end. Things that are valuable merely as means
to some end have only extrinsic value. For example, money has no
intrinsic value, in and of itself. Rather it has extrinsic value insofar as
it's a useful means of commerce for human beings and so is valuable
to us for the ends it helps us achieve. But in and of itself money is
worthless. It's just paper.

Now the question is, are human beings like that, or are they
intrinsically valuable? I'm certain that most people, once they think
about it, recognize that human beings are intrinsically valuable.
People aren't valuable merely as a means to some end; rather people
are ends in themselves. That's why, as Augustine said, we should *love
people* and *use things,* not vice versa. Those who use people and love
things are doing something profoundly immoral, because they are
not recognizing the inherent worth and dignity of other persons, who
are not mere things to be used.

The international community recognizes the intrinsic moral
value of human beings, as expressed in the United Nations'
Universal Declaration of Human Rights. The notion that people have
inherent rights just in virtue of the fact that they are human beings,

regardless of their race, class, religion, caste, or station in life, is based in the inherent moral value of human beings. This truth is recognized as well in the Declaration of Independence, which affirms that all men are endowed with certain unalienable rights, such as the right to life, to liberty, and to the pursuit of happiness. Most of us, when we reflect upon it, would come to a similar conclusion: Yes, human beings do possess intrinsic moral value.

Now what this implies is that if the developing fetus is a human being, then he or she is endowed with intrinsic moral worth and therefore possesses inherent human rights, including the right to life. As the Canadian abortionist Henry Morgentaler concedes, "If indeed there were a human being present from conception, then interfering with its growth or removing it from its human support system would be tantamount to killing a human being."[1] Abortion would be a form of homicide, and against such attacks the innocent and defenseless fetus would have every right to the protection of the law.

So we now come to the second question we must address: *Is the developing fetus a human being?* Here it seems to me that it is virtually undeniable scientifically and medically that the fetus is at every stage of its development a human being. After all, the fetus is not canine, or feline, or bovine; it is a *human* fetus. From the moment of conception on, there exists a living organism which is a genetically complete human being and which, if left to develop naturally, will grow into an adult member of its species. Contrast the complete human embryo with a sperm or an unfertilized egg. Neither the sperm nor the egg alone constitutes a human being: each is genetically incomplete, having only one-half the chromosomes necessary to make a complete human being. If left alone, they don't develop into anything: the sperm dies in a couple of days, and the unfertilized egg is expelled in a woman's monthly cycle. But if they unite, they combine into a single living cell to form a unique individual which has never before existed. Already in that moment of conception, that individual is either male or female, depending on whether he or she

---

[1] Henry Morgentaler, *Abortion and Contraception* (New York: Beaufort, 1982), 143.

received an X or a Y chromosome from the sperm. The later development of sexual organs and other secondary sexual characteristics is only evidence of a difference in sexuality that has been there from the very beginning. Moreover, all of the individual's traits, such as body type, eye and hair color, facial characteristics, and so forth, are determined at the moment of conception and are just waiting to unfold. From the moment of conception we have a genetically complete and unique human being; in effect, *you* began at the moment of your conception.

Moreover, the development of this individual is a smooth and unbroken continuum throughout. There is no nonarbitrary point in the process before which you can say the fetus is not human but after which he or she is. The traditional division of pregnancy into three trimesters has no scientific or medical basis: it is a purely arbitrary reckoning device for the sake of convenience. It is probably due to the fact that pregnancy lasts nine months and 9 is 3x3. If human beings had a gestation time of 8 months, nobody would talk about trimesters! We would probably divide it into quarters. The fact is that any attempt to draw a line and say "not human before this point, but human afterwards" is wholly arbitrary and without biological foundation.

Thus, as I say, it seems virtually undeniable that the fetus—which is just Latin for "little one"—is a human being in the early stages of his development. Whether a "little one," a newborn, an adolescent, or an adult, he is at every point a human being at a different stage of his development.

Those who deny that the little one in the womb is a human being typically confuse *being human* with *being at some later stage of development.* For example, Morgentaler thinks that because an embryo is not a baby, it's not a human being, and therefore abortion is morally acceptable.

This argument seems to me completely fallacious. On this reasoning, we could with equal justice say that because a child is not an adult, he is not a human being; or because a baby is not a child, he is not a human being. Of course, an embryo is not a baby, but that doesn't mean that an embryo is not a human being. All of these are the various stages in a human being's development, and it is completely arbitrary to cut off one stage and say that because it is not a later stage, it is not a human being.

Moreover, it is simply false that abortions are performed on embryos. By the time most pregnancies are detected (about eight weeks into the pregnancy), the embryo has already become a fetus, a "little one." We're not dealing at this point with a cluster of cells, but with—the word is unavoidable—a baby, a very tiny baby with a face and features, with little arms and legs, with tiny feet and hands. All the organs of the body are already present, and the muscle and circulatory systems are complete. Even brain wave activity is present. By the twelfth week, the baby's fingers and toes are fully developed, complete with delicate fingerprints and with little fingernails and toenails forming. The baby is already quite mobile, kicking and moving about, clenching and opening his little fists and curling his toes. Behind his closed eyelids his eyes are almost fully developed. Incredibly, already at this point, the baby's facial features begin to resemble those of his parents!

Fiber-optic photographs of these little ones have disclosed to us what exquisitely beautiful and delicate marvels of creation they are. One physician describes his experience of seeing firsthand one of these eight-week-old little ones:

> Years ago, while giving an anesthetic for a ruptured tubal pregnancy (at two months), I was handed what I believed to be the smallest human being ever seen. The embryo sac was intact and transparent. Within the sac was a tiny human male swimming extremely vigorously in the amniotic fluid, while attached to the wall by the umbilical cord. This tiny human was perfectly developed with long, tapering fingers, feet and toes. It was almost transparent as regards the skin, and the delicate arteries and veins were prominent to the end of the fingers. The baby was extremely alive and did not look at all like the photos and drawings of "embryos" which I have seen. When the sac was opened, the tiny human immediately lost its life and took on the appearance of what is accepted as the appearance of an embryo at this stage, blunt extremities, etc.

No one who has seen photographs of infants in the womb between eight and twelve weeks old can honestly deny that here we have a human baby.

The vast majority of abortions occur at this time, between the tenth and twelfth weeks of pregnancy, and are thus clearly destroying a human baby. I will not even speak of the horror of second- and third-trimester abortions, 150,000 of which occur annually in the United States alone, or of partial birth abortions, in which a baby is actually partially delivered before it is brutally killed. Make no mistake about it: abortion is killing babies. The only way this can go on is because these unlucky little ones are normally hidden from view. As my former pastor once said, "If wombs had windows, there would be no abortions."

In light of these facts, much of the abortion rights rhetoric is seen to be simply absurd. For example, in an interview with *World* magazine, the late Barbara Jordan of the University of Texas recited the abortion rights mantra: "Abortion is a personal choice because you are talking about what a woman does with her body." The incredulous interviewer asked, "Do you reject the understanding that there are actually two bodies involved in an abortion—the mother and the child?" Jordan bit the bullet: "I certainly do. Yes, I do reject the notion."[2]

Now this is just scientific and medical poppycock. The idea that a developing fetus is part of the woman's body is so biologically ignorant that I *would* call it medieval, except that would be to insult the medievals! The fetus is not like an appendix or a gall bladder. From the moment of its conception and implantation in the wall of the mother's uterus, the fetus is *never* a part of her body, but is a biologically distinct and complete living being which is, in effect, "hooked up" to the mother as a life-support system. To say a fetus is part of a woman's body is like saying that a person on life support is part of the iron lung or the intravenous equipment. Having an abortion is not like having an appendectomy. It is killing a separate human being, and

---

[2] Barbara Jordan, quoted in "New Democratic Order?" *World* magazine, November 7, 1992, 8-9.

to try to justify that on the grounds that a woman can do what she wants with her own body is just politically correct ignorance.

The absurd consequences of denying that the little one is a human being were dramatically illustrated by a Connecticut court case reported by the *New York Times*. The case concerned a drug-addicted mother who, just hours before her delivery and after her water had broken, shot up with cocaine while waiting to go to the hospital. This woman had already had one older child removed from her custody by the state because of her drug addiction. But when the state attempted to take custody of the newborn as well, the court intervened to block it because under Connecticut's extremely liberal abortion rights law, the fetus prior to birth was not "a child" and therefore there was nothing illegal about injecting cocaine into its bloodstream. Since the fetus was not a child, the court also declared, neither was the woman a "parent," and therefore her actions could not constitute child abuse. Now I don't need to tell you that this is absolutely insane. How does being expelled through the birth canal magically transform an inhuman entity into a human child? How can we be so blind? The article reported that even the staunchest advocates of abortion rights were uncomfortable about "seeing their philosophy writ so large, with all the implications exposed." Nevertheless, they supported the verdict because, in the words of a Planned Parenthood spokeswoman, the alternative would be to start down the road to denying abortion rights.

She was correct in her logic. What she saw was that if you concede that a fetus is a human being prior to birth, even in the ninth month of pregnancy, then there is no nonarbitrary point in the process where in the human development you can say that before this point the fetus is not human but afterwards it is. And so the cruel logic of the abortion rights position must deny the humanity of these little ones right up to the moment of birth. For that reason abortion rights advocates have been unyielding in their defense of partial birth abortion, in which the baby is delivered feet first until only his head remains inside the birth canal. The doctor then pierces the back of the baby's skull with a pair of surgical scissors and suctions out the baby's brain, causing the skull to collapse before delivery is completed. Because the baby's head remains inside the cervix when he is killed, he is not a human child and so killing him is not homicide.

In fact, the logic of the abortion rights position has driven the hardiest of the abortion activists to oppose legislation protecting babies who have *survived* botched attempts at abortion. What they have clearly seen is that the geographical displacement of the infant from the mother's uterus to the operating table has absolutely no effect upon the human status of the baby, so that if abortion is morally justifiable moments before delivery, infanticide must be justifiable in the time following expulsion. Those congressional supporters of abortion rights who caved on partial birth abortion have permitted the crack in the dike of the abortion rights position.

The fact is that from conception to old age we have the various stages of development in the life of a human being. It seems therefore that the medical and scientific facts make it virtually undeniable that the developing fetus is a human being.

If we thus answer "Yes" to both of the questions we've set ourselves, it follows that abortion is a moral outrage, the destruction of an innocent and defenseless human life.

Confronted with the undeniable scientific facts about fetal development, some abortion rights proponents suddenly begin to backpedal at this point. "Wait a minute," they say, "we didn't really mean that all human beings have intrinsic moral value. Rather *persons* do, where 'person' means a self-conscious individual. Since the fetus is not a person in this sense, it has no intrinsic moral value and so there's nothing wrong with killing it."

But it seems to me that this proposed escape route will not work and even has sinister consequences. First, even if the little one in the womb were not a person, he or she is still a potential person and in that respect differs crucially from, say, the fetus of a dog or a cat. The little one will eventually become a self-conscious individual, and it's not at all clear that we have the right to prevent this potentiality from being actualized by killing him.

Second, more fundamentally, the proposed view fails to distinguish between *being* a person and *functioning* as a person. If self-consciousness is necessary to being a person, then someone who is asleep or in a coma is not a person, which is absurd. If you cease to be a person when you fall asleep, then there's nothing wrong with someone's killing you in your sleep. (They just have to be real quick about it, or they might wake you up and then you would become a person again and killing you would be murder!) This makes it clear that there is a difference between *being* a person and *functioning* as a person. When you're asleep you're still a person; you're just not, at that moment, functioning as a person. But then on what grounds do we know that a little one in the womb is not also a person, but is just not yet functioning as a person? I can think of no way of proving that babies *in utero* are not already persons, who in time will begin to function as self-conscious individuals. If this is so, they are not potential persons; rather they are persons with potential.

Third, the decisive refutation of the proposed view is that it also serves to justify infanticide. For newborn babies are not self-conscious individuals either, and so, under the proposed definition, are not persons. Thus, if abortion is justified, so is infanticide. Some proponents of abortion rights, again forced by the cruel logic of their position, have publicly endorsed infanticide. The Nobel laureate James D. Watson wrote in 1973,

> If a child were not declared alive until three days after birth, then all parents could be allowed the choice only few are given under the present system. The doctor could allow the child to die if the parents so choose and save a lot of misery and suffering. I believe this view is the only rational, compassionate attitude to have.[3]

But, of course, three days is not long enough for a newborn to develop self-consciousness. A year, maybe two, will be necessary. All during this time, the child is not a person and so can be killed off, like putting an unwanted pet to sleep. Surely anyone whose heart has not been utterly hardened by an obsessive commitment to abortion on

[3] James D. Watson, "Children from the Laboratory," *Prism* (May 1973).

demand will recognize the terrible immorality and hence unaccept-
ability of this proposed escape route!

Now you'll notice that I haven't appealed at any point to the Bible
in all this. That's because, contrary to popular impression, abortion is
not as such a religious question. The first question we asked is philosophical: do human beings posses intrinsic moral value? The second
question is scientific and medical: is the developing fetus a human
being? Neither of these is a religious question. That's why among the
strongest opponents of abortion are humanists, like the late Dr. Bernard
Nathanson, a former abortionist himself. As a humanist he believed that
human beings are intrinsically valuable and as a doctor he could no
longer deny the evident humanity of his victims. So he renounced his
practice and came to oppose abortion as a terrible evil.

But why do the vast majority of the opponents of abortion seem
to be Christians? The answer is because Christians also have *biblical*
reasons for answering "Yes" to both of the questions I raised. With
respect to the first question, the Bible declares that man—both male
and female—is made in the image of God (Gen. 1:27). Because of
this, human beings are intrinsically valuable and possess certain God-
given rights. The biblical prohibition of murder is based specifically
in the fact that man is created in God's image (Gen. 9:6). The second
greatest commandment is that we should love our neighbor, and this
is a universal command extending to every human being. Not only
this, but every human being is a person for whom Christ died, which
gives each person unspeakable value. On the Christian worldview,
then, one single human being is worth more than the entire material
universe. Because of their exalted view of man, Christians are deeply
committed to the cause of human rights.

With respect to the second question, the Bible also suggests that
human life begins not at birth but in the womb. There are a surprising number of biblical references to life in the womb. Some forty
times the Scripture refers to conception as the start of new life in the
womb. Moreover, God is represented as caring about and even calling people while they are in the womb. For example, look at Psalm
139:13-16 (ESV):

For you formed my inward parts;
> you knitted me together in my mother's womb.
I praise you, for I am fearfully and wonderfully made.
Wonderful are your works;
> my soul knows it very well.
My frame was not hidden from you,
when I was being made in secret,
> intricately woven in the depths of the earth.
Your eyes saw my unformed substance;
in your book were written, every one of them,
> the days that were formed for me,
when as yet there were none of them.

Here the psalmist describes how God knew and created him in his mother's womb. Especially noteworthy is his declaration that even in the womb God had a plan for his life, which included the entire course of his life until the day of his death. As God beheld this "little one" in his mother's womb, He already had in mind plans and purposes and projects to be accomplished through that life.

A similar theme is sounded by the prophet Jeremiah:

Now the word of the Lord came to me, saying,

"Before I formed you in the womb I knew you,
> and before you were born I consecrated you;
> I appointed you a prophet to the nations" (1:4-5, ESV).

Here again we see God's involvement in the life of the unborn and His plan for this person's life.

When we read such passages, it is hardly surprising that abortion was never practiced among the Jews. There was no need for a specific commandment against killing the unborn, just as there was no need for a commandment against killing one's wife; both were implicitly comprised under the single commandment, "Thou shalt not kill."

Thus, Christians have biblical grounds, as well as philosophical and scientific grounds, for affirming the value of human life and the humanity of the unborn, and therefore—thank God—they have been in the forefront of opposition to this terrible slaughter of the innocents. But abortion isn't a religious issue *per se*. For that reason, when we Christians try to affect public policy on this issue, we would be wise not to base our argument on biblical grounds, which in our post-Christian culture have no force for non-Christians who reject the Bible, but on general humanitarian grounds that appeal to all people.

In the same way, I think it is clear from what I've said that neither is abortion a gender issue. Radical feminists have latched on to abortion on demand as a symbol of all that women's rights embodies. Hence, some feminists have an obsessive, even fanatical, commitment to abortion. But such an equation of abortion rights with women's rights is wholly mistaken. Abortion is not a gender issue; it's an ethical issue: Does anyone have the right to take an innocent human life? One can and should be committed to equal opportunity for women in the marketplace, to equal pay for equal work, and so forth, without illogically inferring from that that one has the right to destroy innocent human life.

The mention of women's issues raises a further point: a consistent pro-life position is not just anti-abortion. It is also pro-mother and pro-child and advocates that there be available to women a range of social services which make carrying pregnancy to term practicable—things like pregnancy counseling, day care, medical benefits, adoption services, and so forth. We need to help women see that they are not forced to have an abortion, but that alternatives are available.

Now, as I say, how you answer the two fundamental questions I've addressed will pretty much determine everything else in the abortion debate. For once you see that human life is intrinsically valuable and that we are dealing here with human lives, then virtually all of the arguments in favor of abortion on demand become obviously unsound. Take, for example, the arguments which the former member of my church offered in her letter:

1. *Murder must have a malicious motive.* We may grant the premise if we wish, but that doesn't imply that abortion is justified. Even if abor-

tion is not murder-so-defined, it is still homicide, and the killing of innocent human beings is wrong.

2. *There are too many unwanted children in the world, and white couples don't like to adopt minority children.* Suppose we grant the premise just for the sake of argument. What follows? That we should kill off the children before they're born? Is it morally justified to kill an innocent human being because he's not wanted? That's crazy. What we should do is to expand availability of and education about methods of contraception which do not involve the destruction of a fertilized egg, and foster programs to make adoption easier.

This argument also contains a subtle undertone of racism that I find very disturbing: abortion is needed, the argument seems to be saying, to control all those Asians and black Africans whose populations are growing too fast. Let them kill off their unborn babies and keep themselves in check! Needless to say, such an attitude should be anathema to any Christian.

Finally, let me say that the argument is really naive: families in many Third World countries are large, not because children are *un*wanted, but precisely because they *are* wanted to take care of the parents when they're old. With high infant mortality rates, poverty, and disease, one's chances of having someone to care for you when you're old are better if you have lots of children. Abortion on demand solves nothing. What has to be done is to attack the poverty and disease that lie at the root of the problem.

3. *The world's population is exploding too rapidly.* Again, this doesn't justify killing off innocent human beings. The logical implication of this objection is population control in which the weak and the unwanted are killed off to make room for the strong. The morally appropriate response to population growth is better birth control, not killing innocent people.

4. *Most childless couples don't want to have children or adopt.* Even if this were true, it wouldn't justify killing innocent human beings. Besides, I suspect that this is sheer opinion with no basis in fact. In our own family, my two brothers-in-law and their wives are just two examples of couples who went through agony trying to have children of their

own. In any case, the objection is irrelevant. Many families who already have children choose to adopt. Our neighbors down the street have just done this. The fact is that there are millions of people waiting to adopt children and no shortage of loving families for the would-be victims of abortion.

5. *A woman's body is her own business; it should not be a political issue.* We've already seen that in abortion two bodies, two human beings, are involved. As to whose business it is, Abraham Lincoln once described the purpose of government as being "to help those who cannot help themselves." There is no one more helpless and defenseless than an unborn child; they deserve the protection of the law. So whose business is it? Here I recall the words of Marley's ghost in Charles Dickens's *A Christmas Carol.* When Scrooge assures him, "You were always a good man at business, Jacob," the ghost cries, "Business! Mankind was my business!" The same is true today. The blood of millions of innocent children cries out to God, and Christians, of all people, cannot dare to turn a deaf and callous ear toward their cry.

6. *If people in underdeveloped nations are urged to have birth control or abortion, the same policies should apply in developed nations.* The answer, of course, is that no nation should be urged to carry out abortions. Abortion is a moral abomination that is a disgrace to any people.

Do you see what I mean? Once you grant that human beings have intrinsic moral value and that the unborn are human beings, the rest falls into place. There is simply no justification for the undeclared war being waged against the unborn.

Now what practical application does all this have for us? What should and can we do?

First of all, if you should have an unwanted pregnancy, *do not have an abortion.* It may be hard to accommodate yourself to bearing an unexpected child, but think of what you are doing. If you choose abortion, you are killing your son or your daughter. *Do not do such a heinous thing.* If you have already had an abortion and perhaps are struggling with secret guilt, then know that there is forgiveness and cleansing with the Lord if you confess your sin and turn to Him in repentance and faith.

Similarly, if your unmarried daughter should—God forbid— become pregnant, *do not encourage her to seek an abortion.* Two wrongs will not make a right. One mistake is bad enough; do not compound it further by having her commit homicide against her own daughter or son.

Second, if you know of someone who is contemplating abortion, do all you can to persuade that person not to kill her own baby. Get some pamphlets for expectant mothers showing pictures of fetal development and help her to see clearly what abortion does to her baby. Offer her emotional support and help to make the right decision. In so doing you will not only help her but you will save a human life.

Finally, become politically involved to change abortion laws where possible. Familiarize yourself with the issues, for example, by receiving the National Right to Life newspaper. Vote for elected officials based on their pro-life stance. Speak out against the promotion of abortion in your children's schools or wherever the issue is raised.

Every year millions of babies are destroyed through abortion. Let us raise our voices in protest against this slaughter of the unborn. Is this "right wing religious propaganda"? Hardly. It is a philosophically and scientifically informed ethical concern. But there's a better word for it: it's called *compassion.* God help us if our hearts have grown so cold that we cannot weep for these little ones who perish daily by the thousands.

7

HOMOSEXUALITY

One of the most volatile and important issues facing the church today is the question of homosexuality as an alternative lifestyle. The church cannot duck this question. Events like the brutal murder of Matthew Shepherd, the homosexual student in Wyoming, or the recent spate of scandals involving pedophile priests, which has rocked the Catholic Church, serve to thrust this question to the front and center.

Christians who reject the legitimacy of the homosexual lifestyle are routinely denounced as homophobic, intolerant, even hateful. There is thus tremendous intimidation concerning this issue. Some churches have even endorsed the homosexual lifestyle and welcome those who practice it to be their ministers.

And don't think this is happening just in liberal churches. One homosexual organization called Evangelicals Concerned is a group of people who are to all appearances born-again, Bible-believing Christians, but also practicing homosexuals. They claim either that the Bible doesn't forbid homosexual activity or that its commands aren't valid for today but were just a reflection of the culture in when it was written. These people can be orthodox about Jesus and every other area of teaching; but they just think it's all right to be a practicing homosexual. I recall hearing a New Testament scholar at a professional conference relate the story of his speaking in one of their meetings. "Folks were really concerned about what you were going to say," his host said after the meeting. "Why?" he asked in surprise. "You know I'm not homophobic!" "Oh, no, that wasn't the concern," his host reassured him. "They were afraid you'd be too historical-critical!"

So who are we to say these apparently earnest Christians are wrong?

Now that's a *very* good question. Who are we to say that they are wrong? But this question raises an even deeper question, which we've got to answer first: do right and wrong really exist? Before you can determine *what* is right and wrong, you have to know that there really is right and wrong.

Well, what is the basis for saying that right and wrong exist, that there really is a difference between these two? Traditionally, the answer has been that moral values are based in God. God is by His very nature perfectly holy and good. He is just, loving, patient, merciful, generous—all that is good comes from Him and is a reflection of His character. Now God's perfectly good nature issues forth in commandments to us, which become our moral duties: for example, "You shall love the Lord your God with all your heart, mind, and strength," "You shall love your neighbor as yourself," "You shall not murder, steal, or commit adultery." These things are right or wrong based on God's commandments, and God's commandments are not arbitrary but flow necessarily out of His perfect nature.

This is the Christian understanding of right and wrong. There really is such a being as God, who created the world and made us to know Him. He really has commanded certain things. We really are morally obligated to do certain things (and not to do others). Morality isn't just in your mind. It's real. When we fail to keep God's commandments, we really are morally guilty before Him and need His forgiveness. The problem isn't just that we *feel* guilty; we really *are* guilty, regardless of how we feel. If I have an insensitive conscience, one that's dulled by sin, I might not *feel* guilty; but if I've broken God's law, I *am* guilty, regardless of how I feel.

So, for example, if the Nazis had won World War II and succeeded in brainwashing or exterminating everyone who disagreed with them, so that everybody would think the Holocaust had been good, it would still have been wrong, because God says it is wrong, regardless of human opinion. Morality is based in God, and so real right and wrong exist and are unaffected by human opinions.

I've emphasized this point because it's so foreign to what a lot of people in our society think today. Today so many people think of right and wrong, not as matters of *fact,* but as matters of *taste.* There isn't any objective fact, for example, that *broccoli tastes good.* It tastes good to some people, but tastes bad to others. It may taste bad to you, but it tastes good to me! People think it's the same with moral values. Something may be wrong for you, but right for me. There isn't any real right or wrong. It's just a matter of opinion.

Now if there is no God, then I think these people are absolutely correct. In the absence of God everything becomes relative. Right and wrong become relative to different cultures and societies. Without God, who is to say that one culture's values are better than another's? Who's to say who is right and who is wrong? Where would right and wrong come from? Richard Taylor, who is a prominent American philosopher—and not a Christian, by the way—makes this point very forcefully. Look carefully at what he says:

> The idea of moral obligation is clear enough, provided that reference to some higher lawmaker is understood. In other words, our moral obligations can be understood as those that are imposed by God. But what if this higher-than-human lawmaker is no longer taken into account? Does the concept of a moral obligation still make sense?[1]

He says the answer is "No." I quote: "The concept of moral obligation is unintelligible apart from the idea of God. The words remain, but their meaning is gone."[2] He goes on to say:

> The modern age, more or less repudiating the idea of a divine lawgiver, has nevertheless tried to retain the ideas of moral right and

[1] Richard Taylor, *Ethics, Faith, and Reason* (Englewood Cliffs, N.J.: Prentice-Hall, 1985), 83.
[2] Ibid., 84.

wrong, without noticing that in casting God aside they have also abolished the meaningfulness of right and wrong as well. Thus, even educated persons sometimes declare that such things as war, or abortion, or the violation of certain human rights are morally wrong, and they imagine that they have said something true and meaningful. Educated people do not need to be told, however, that questions such as these have never been answered outside of religion.[3]

Do you catch what even this non-Christian philosopher is saying? If there is no God, no divine lawgiver, then there is no moral law. If there is no moral law, then there is no real right and wrong. Right and wrong are just human customs and conventions that vary from society to society. Even if they all agree, they're still just human inventions.

So if God does not exist, right and wrong do not exist either. Anything goes, including homosexuality. So one of the best ways to defend the legitimacy of the homosexual lifestyle is to become an atheist. But the problem is that many defenders of homosexuality don't want to become atheists. In particular, they do want to affirm that right and wrong exist. So you hear them making moral judgments all the time, for example: "It is wrong to discriminate against homosexuals." And these moral judgments aren't meant to be just relative to a culture or society. They would condemn a society like Nazi Germany which threw homosexuals into concentration camps, along with Jews and other undesirables. When Colorado passed an amendment prohibiting special rights for homosexuals, Barbara Streisand called for a boycott of the state, saying that the state's moral climate had become "unacceptable."

But we've seen that these kinds of value judgments cannot be meaningfully made unless God exists. If God does not exist, anything goes, including discrimination and persecution of homosexuals. But it doesn't stop there: murder, rape, torture, child abuse—none of these things would be wrong, because without God right and wrong do not exist. Everything is permitted.

<hr>

[3] Ibid., 2-3.

So if we want to be able to make moral judgments about what's right or wrong, we've got to affirm that God exists. But then the same question we started with—"Who are you to say that homosexuality is wrong?"—can be put back to homosexual activists: "Who are you to say that homosexuality is *right?*" If God exists, then we cannot ignore what *He* has to say about the subject. The correct answer to the "Who are you to say . . . ?" question is to reply, "Me? I'm nobody! God determines what's right and wrong, and I'm just interested in learning and obeying what He says."

So let me recap what we've seen so far. The question of the legitimacy of the homosexual lifestyle is a question of what God has to say about it. If there is no God, then there is no right and wrong, and it doesn't make any difference what lifestyle you choose—and the persecutor of homosexuals is equal to the advocate of homosexuality. But if God does exist, we can no longer go just on the basis of our own opinions. We have to find out what God thinks on the issue.

So how do you find out what God thinks? The Christian says, you look in the Bible. And the Bible tells us that God forbids homosexual acts. Therefore, they are wrong.

So basically the reasoning goes like this:

(1) We are all obligated to do God's will.
(2) God's will is expressed in the Bible.
(3) The Bible forbids homosexual behavior.
(4) Therefore, homosexual behavior is against God's will, or
    is wrong.

Now if someone is going to resist this reasoning, he's got to deny either that (2) God's will is expressed in the Bible or else that (3) the Bible forbids homosexual behavior.

Let's look at point (3) first: Does the Bible in fact forbid homosexual behavior? Now notice how I put that question. I did not ask, Does the Bible forbid homosexuality? but rather, Does the Bible forbid homosexual *behavior?* This is an important distinction. Being homosexual is a state or an orientation; a person who has a homosexual orientation might not ever express that orientation in actions. By contrast, a person could engage in homosexual acts even if he has a heterosexual orientation. What the Bible condemns is homosexual actions or behavior, not having a homosexual orientation. The idea of a person's being a homosexual by orientation is a feature of modern psychology and may have been unknown to people in the ancient world. What they were familiar with was homosexual acts, and this is what the Bible forbids.

Now this has enormous implications. For one thing, it means that the whole debate about whether homosexuality is something you were born with or is a result of how you were raised really doesn't matter in the end. The important thing is not how you *got* your orientation, but what you *do* with it. Some defenders of homosexuality are very anxious to prove that your genes, not your upbringing, determine if you're homosexual—because then homosexual behavior is normal and right. But this conclusion doesn't follow at all. Just because you're genetically disposed to some behavior doesn't mean that the behavior is morally right. To give an example, some researchers suspect there may be a gene that predisposes some people to alcoholism. Does that mean that it's all right for someone with such predisposition to go ahead and drink to his heart's content and become an alcoholic? Obviously not! If anything, it ought to alert him to *abstain* from alcohol so as to prevent this from happening. Now the sober truth of the matter is that we don't fully understand the roles of heredity and environment in producing homosexuality. But that doesn't really matter. Even if homosexuality were completely genetic, that fact alone still wouldn't make it any different than a birth defect, like a cleft palate or epilepsy. It doesn't mean it's normal and that we shouldn't try to correct it.

In any case, whether homosexuality results from genetics or from upbringing, people don't generally choose to be homosexual. Many homosexuals testify how agonizing it is to find yourself with these desires and to fight against them, and they'll tell you they would never choose to be that way. And the Bible doesn't condemn a person because he has a homosexual orientation. What it condemns is homosexual acts. It is perfectly possible to be a homosexual and be a born-again, Spirit-filled Christian.

Just as an alcoholic who is dry will still stand up at an AA meeting and say, "I am an alcoholic," so a homosexual who is living straight and keeping himself pure ought to be able to stand up in a prayer meeting and say, "I am a homosexual. But by God's grace and by the power of the Holy Spirit, I'm living chastely for Christ." And I hope we would have the courage and love to welcome him or her as a brother or sister in Christ.

So, once more, the question is: Does the Bible forbid homosexual behavior? Well, I've already said that it does. The Bible is so realistic! You might not expect it to mention a topic like homosexual behavior, but in fact there are six places in the Bible—three in the Old Testament and three in the New Testament—where this issue is directly addressed—not to mention all the passages dealing with marriage and sexuality which have implications for this issue. In all six of these passages homosexual acts are unequivocally condemned.

Leviticus 18:22 says that it is an abomination for a man to lie with another man as with a woman. In Leviticus 20:13 the death penalty is prescribed in Israel for such an act, along with adultery, incest, and bestiality. Now sometimes homosexual advocates make light of these prohibitions by comparing them to prohibitions in the Old Testament against unclean animals like pigs. Just as Christians today don't obey all of the Old Testament ceremonial laws, so, they say, we don't have to obey the prohibitions of homosexual actions. But the problem with this argument is that the New Testament reaffirms the validity of the Old Testament prohibitions of homosexual behavior, as we'll see below. This shows the prohibitions were not just part of the ceremonial laws of the Old Testament, which were done away with, but were part of God's everlasting moral law. Homosexual behavior is in God's sight a serious sin. The third place where homosexual acts are mentioned in the Old Testament is the horrifying story in Genesis 19 of the attempted gang rape of Lot's visitors by the men of Sodom, from which our word *sodomy* derives. God destroyed the city of Sodom because of their wickedness.

If this were not enough, the New Testament also forbids homosexual behavior. In 1 Corinthians 6:9-10 (ESV) Paul writes, "Do you
not know that the unrighteous will not inherit the kingdom of God?
Do not be deceived: neither the sexually immoral, nor idolaters, nor
adulterers, nor men who practice homosexuality, nor thieves, nor the
greedy, nor drunkards, nor revilers, nor swindlers will inherit the
kingdom of God." The words in the list translated "men who practice homosexuality" refer in Greek literature to both the passive and
the active partners in male homosexual intercourse. (As I said, the
Bible is very realistic!) The second of these two words is also listed in
1 Timothy 1:10 along with fornicators, slave traders, liars, and mur-
derers as "contrary" to the sound teaching of the gospel. The most
lengthy treatment of homosexual activity comes in Romans 1:24-28.
Here Paul talks about how people have turned away from the Creator
God and have begun to worship instead false gods of their own making. He says (ESV),

> Therefore God gave them up in the lusts of their hearts to impu-
> rity, to the dishonoring of their bodies among themselves, because
> they exchanged the truth about God for a lie and worshipped and
> served the creature rather than the Creator, who is blessed forever!
> Amen.
>
> For this reason God gave them up to dishonorable passions. For
> their women exchanged natural relations for those that are contrary
> to nature; and the men likewise gave up natural relations with
> women and were consumed with passion for one another, men
> committing shameless acts with men and receiving in themselves
> the due penalty for their error.

Liberal scholars have done acrobatics to try to explain away the
clear sense of these verses. Some have said that Paul is only condemning the pagan practice of men sexually exploiting young boys.
But such an interpretation is obviously wrong, since Paul says in
verses 24 and 27 that these homosexual acts by men were committed
"with one another" and in verse 26 he speaks of lesbian homosexual

acts as well. Other scholars have said Paul is only condemning *hetero-sexuals* who engage in homosexual acts, not homosexuals who do. But this interpretation is contrived and anachronistic. We've already said that it was only in modern times that the idea of homosexual or het-erosexual *orientation* developed. What Paul is condemning is homo-sexual acts, regardless of orientation. Given the Old Testament background to this passage as well as what Paul says in 1 Corinthians 6:9-10 and 1 Timothy 1:10, it is clear that Paul is here forbidding all such acts. He sees this behavior as the evidence of a corrupted mind that has turned away from God and has been abandoned by Him to moral degeneracy.

So the Bible is very forthright and clear when it comes to homo-sexual behavior. It is contrary to God's design and is sin. Even if there weren't all these explicit passages dealing with homosexual acts, such acts would still be forbidden under the commandment "You shall not commit adultery." God's plan for human sexual activity is that it is reserved for marriage: any sexual activity outside of the security of the marriage bond—whether premarital sex or extramarital sex, whether heterosexual or homosexual—is forbidden. Sex is designed by God for marriage.

Someone might say that if God intended sex for marriage, then just let homosexuals marry each other and they would not be com-mitting adultery! But this suggestion completely misunderstands God's intention for marriage. The creation story in Genesis tells of how God made woman as a suitable mate for man, his perfect, God-given complement. Then it says, "For this reason a man will leave his father and mother and be united to his wife, and they will become one flesh" (Gen. 2:24). This is God's pattern for marriage, and in the New Testament Paul quotes this very passage and then says, "This is a profound mystery—but I am talking about Christ and the church" (Eph. 5:32). Paul says that the union between a man and his wife is a living symbol of the unity of Christ with His people, the church. When we think about this, we can see what a terrible sacrilege, what a mockery of God's plan, a homosexual union is. It flies in the face of God's intention for humanity from the moment of creation.

The above also shows how silly it is when some homosexual advocates say, "Jesus never condemned homosexual behavior, so why should we?" Jesus did not specifically mention lots of things that we know to be wrong, like bestiality or torture, but that doesn't mean He *approved* of them. What Jesus does do is quote from Genesis to affirm God's pattern for marriage as the basis for His own teaching on divorce. In Mark 10:6-8, He says, "But at the beginning of creation God 'made them male and female.' 'For this reason a man will leave his father and mother and be united to his wife, and the two will become one flesh.' So they are no longer two, but one." For two men to become one flesh in homosexual intercourse would be a violation of God's created order and intent. He created man and woman, not two men or two women, to be indissolubly united in marriage.

To recap, then, the Bible clearly and consistently forbids homosexual activity. So if God's will is expressed in the Bible, it follows that homosexual behavior is against God's will.

But suppose someone denies point (2), that God's will is expressed in the Bible? Suppose he says that the prohibitions against homosexual behavior were valid for that time and that culture but are no longer valid today? After all, most of us would probably agree that certain commands in the Bible are relative to the culture. For example, the Bible says that Christian women should not wear jewelry and men should not have long hair. But most of us would say that while these commands do have a timelessly valid core—like, say, the injunction to dress modestly—that core principle may be differently expressed in different cultures. In the same way, some people are saying that the Bible's prohibitions against homosexual behavior are no longer valid for our day and age.

But I think this objection represents a serious misunderstanding. There's no evidence that Paul's commands concerning homosexual acts are culturally relative. Far from being a reflection of the culture in which he wrote, Paul's commands are downright countercultural! Homosexual activity was as widespread in ancient Greek and Roman society as it is today in the United States, and yet Paul stood up against the culture and opposed it. More importantly, we've seen that the Bible's prohibitions against homosexual activity are rooted, not in culture, but in the God-given pattern for marriage established at creation. You can't deny that the Bible's forbidding homosexual relations expresses God's will unless you also reject that marriage itself expresses God's will.

Well, suppose someone goes the whole way and says, "I believe in God, but not the God of the Bible. So I don't believe the Bible expresses God's will." What do you say to such a person?

It seems to me that there are two ways to respond. First, you could try to show that God has revealed Himself in the Bible. This is the task of Christian apologetics. You could talk about the evidence for the resurrection of Jesus or fulfilled prophecy. Scripture actually commands us as believers to have such a defense ready to share with anyone who should ask us about why we believe as we do (1 Pet. 3:15).

Or secondly, you could try to show that homosexual behavior is wrong by appealing to generally accepted moral truths that even people who don't believe in the Bible accept. While this approach is more difficult, nevertheless I think that it is crucial if we as Christians are to have an impact on our contemporary culture. We are living in a society that is more and more secular, more and more post-Christian. We can't just appeal to the Bible if we're going to influence lawmakers or public schools or other institutions, because most people don't believe in the Bible anymore. We need to give reasons that have a broader appeal.

For example, I think many people would agree with the principle that it's wrong to engage in self-destructive behavior. For such behavior destroys a human being who is inherently valuable. Thus, many people, I think, would say that it is wrong to become an alcoholic or a chain-smoker. They would say that it's good to eat right and stay fit. Moreover, I think almost everybody would agree with the principle that it's wrong to engage in behavior that hurts another person. For example, we restrict smoking to certain areas or ban it altogether so that other people won't have to inhale secondhand smoke, and we pass laws against drunk driving so that innocent people won't be hurt. Almost everybody agrees that you have no right to engage in a behavior that is destructive to another human being.

But it's not hard to show that homosexual behavior is one of the most self-destructive and harmful behaviors a person could engage in. This fact is not widely publicized. Hollywood and the media are relentlessly bent on putting a happy face on homosexuality, whereas in fact it is a dark, twisted, and dangerous lifestyle, just as addictive and destructive as alcoholism or smoking. The sobering statistics I'm about to share with you are all fully documented by Dr. Thomas Schmidt in his remarkable book *Straight and Narrow?*[4]

To begin with, there is an almost compulsive promiscuity associated with homosexual behavior. Seventy-five percent of homosexual men have more than 100 sexual partners during their lifetime. More than half of these partners are strangers. Only 8 percent of homosexual men and 7 percent of homosexual women ever have relationships lasting more than three years. Nobody knows the reason for this strange, obsessive promiscuity. It may be that homosexuals are trying to satisfy a deep psychological need by sexual encounters, and it just is not fulfilling. Male homosexuals average more than 20 partners a year. According to Dr. Schmidt,

> . . . the number of homosexual men who experience anything like lifelong fidelity becomes, statistically speaking, almost meaningless.
>
> Promiscuity among homosexual men is not a mere stereotype, and it is not merely the majority experience—it is virtually the *only* experience. . . . lifelong faithfulness is almost non-existent in the homosexual experience.[5]

Associated with this compulsive promiscuity is widespread drug use by homosexuals to heighten their sexual experiences. Homosexuals in general are three times more likely than the general population to be problem drinkers. Studies show that 47 percent of

---

[4] Thomas E. Schmidt, *Straight and Narrow?* (Downer's Gove, Ill.: InterVarsity Press, 1995), chapter 6.
[5] Ibid., 108.

male homosexuals have a history of alcohol abuse and 51 percent have a history of drug abuse. There is a direct correlation between the number of partners and the amount of drugs consumed.

Moreover, according to Schmidt, "There is overwhelming evidence that certain mental disorders occur with much higher frequency among homosexuals."[6] For example, 40 percent of homosexual men have a history of major depression. That compares with only 3 percent for men in general. Similarly 37 percent of female homosexuals have a history of depression. This leads in turn to heightened suicide rates. Homosexuals are three times as likely to contemplate suicide as the general population. In fact homosexual men have an attempted suicide rate six times that of heterosexual men, and homosexual women attempt suicide twice as often as heterosexual women. Nor are depression and suicide the only problems. Studies show that homosexuals are much more likely to be pedophiles than heterosexual men. Whatever the causes of these disorders, the fact remains that anyone contemplating a homosexual lifestyle should have no illusions about what he is getting into.

Another well-kept secret is how physically dangerous homosexual behavior is. I'm not going to describe the kinds of sexual activity practiced by homosexuals, but just let me say that our bodies, male and female, are designed for sexual intercourse in a way that two male bodies are not. As a result, homosexual activity, 80 percent of which is carried out by men, is very destructive, resulting eventually in such problems as prostate damage, ulcers and ruptures, and chronic incontinence and diarrhea.

In addition to these physical problems, sexually transmitted diseases are rampant among the homosexual population. Seventy-five percent of homosexual men carry one or more sexually transmitted diseases, *wholly apart* from AIDS. These include all sorts of nonviral infections like gonorrhea, syphilis, bacterial infections, and parasites. Also common among homosexuals are viral infections like herpes

---

[6] Ibid., 113.

and hepatitis B (which afflicts 65 percent of homosexual men), both of which are incurable, as well as hepatitis A and anal warts, which afflict 40 percent of homosexual men. And I haven't even included AIDS. Perhaps the most shocking and frightening statistic is that, leaving aside those who die from AIDS, the life expectancy for a homosexual male is about 45 years. That compares to a life expectancy of around 70 for men in general. If you include those who die of AIDS, which now infects 30 percent of homosexual men, the life expectancy drops to *39 years.*

So I think a very good case can be made on the basis of generally accepted moral principles that homosexual behavior is wrong. It is horribly self-destructive and injurious to another person. Thus, wholly apart from the Bible's prohibition, there are sound, sensible reasons to regard homosexual activity as wrong.

Now this has very important implications for public policy concerning homosexual behavior. For public laws and policies are based on such generally accepted moral principles. That's why, for example, we have laws regulating the sale of alcohol in various ways or laws prohibiting gambling or regulations that restrict smoking. These restrictions on individual freedom are imposed for the general good. In the same way, some states, like our home state of Georgia, have laws prohibiting sodomy. Though such a law is undoubtedly unenforceable, it might be deemed justifiable in light of the health risks posed by such behavior.

Now in other cases, enforceable laws governing homosexuality might be proposed, and Christians will have to think hard about these on an individual basis. For example, a Christian might not see any good reason why equal opportunity in buying or renting housing should not be guaranteed to persons who are homosexuals. But I could well imagine that a Christian might oppose a bill guaranteeing equal employment opportunities for homosexuals. For some jobs might be inappropriate for such persons. For example, would you want a practicing lesbian to be your daughter's physical education teacher at school? Would you want your son's coach, who would be in the locker room with the boys, to be a homosexual? I, for one, would not support a law which could force public schools to hire such individuals.

Or again, should health classes in public schools teach that homosexuality is a legitimate lifestyle. Should students be given reading like *Heather Has Two Mommies*? Should homosexual unions be recognized as being on a legal par with heterosexual marriages? Should homosexuals be allowed to adopt children? In all these cases, one might argue for restrictions on homosexual liberties on the basis of the general public good and health. This is not a matter of imposing one's personal values on others, since it is based on the same general moral principles that are used, for example, to ban drug use or pass gun laws. Liberty does not mean the license to engage in actions that hurt other people.

To sum up, we've seen, first, that right and wrong are real because they are based in God. So if we want to find out what is right or wrong, we should look at what God says about it. Second, we saw that the Bible consistently and clearly forbids homosexual acts, just as it does all sexual acts outside of marriage. Third, we saw that the Bible's prohibition of such behavior can't be explained away as just the reflection of the time and culture in which it was written, because it is grounded in God's divine plan for man-woman marriage. Moreover, even apart from the Bible, there are generally accepted moral principles that imply that homosexual behavior is wrong.

Now what practical application does all this have for us as individuals?

First, if you are a homosexual or feel that inclination, keep yourself pure. You should practice abstinence from all sexual activity. I know this is difficult, but really what God is asking you to do is pretty much the same thing that He requires of *all* single people. That means keeping not only your body pure, but especially your mind. Just as heterosexual men should avoid pornography and fantasizing, you, too, need to keep your thought-life clean. Resist the temptation to rationalize sin by saying, "God made me this way." God has made it very clear that He does not want you to indulge your desires, but to honor Him by keeping your mind and body pure. Finally, seek professional Christian counseling. With time and effort, you can come to enjoy normal, heterosexual relations. There is hope.

Second, for those of us who are heterosexual, we need to remember that being homosexual, as such, is no sin. Most homosexuals did not choose such an orientation and would like to change it if they could. We need to accept and lovingly support brothers and sisters who are struggling with this problem. And in general, we need to extend God's love and forgiveness to homosexual people. Vulgar words or jokes about homosexuals should never pass the lips of a Christian. If you find yourself feeling glad when some affliction befalls a homosexual person or you find feelings of hatred welling up in your heart toward homosexual people, then you need to reflect long and hard on the words of Jesus recorded in Matthew: "it will be more tolerable on the day of judgment for Sodom and Gomorrah than for you" (see Matt. 10:15; 11:24, RSV).

8

CHRIST,
THE ONLY WAY

Salvation is found in no one else, for there is no other name under heaven given to men by which we must be saved" (Acts 4:12). Thus the earliest apostles of Christ believed, and thus they preached. That name they preached was, of course, the name of Jesus of Nazareth, and it was through Him and Him alone that salvation was to be found. Indeed, this conviction permeates the New Testament and helped to spur the mission to the Gentiles. Paul invited his Gentile converts to recall their pre-Christian days: "Remember that at that time you were separated from Christ, excluded from citizenship in Israel, and foreigners to the covenants of the promise, without hope and without God in the world" (Eph. 2:12).

The burden of the opening chapters of Romans is to show that this desolate situation is the general condition of mankind. Although God's eternal power and deity are evident through creation (Rom. 1:20) and although God offers eternal life to all who seek Him in well-doing (2:7), the tragic fact of the matter is that in general people suppress the truth in unrighteousness, ignoring the Creator (1:18-21) and flouting the moral law (1:32). Therefore, "Jews and Gentiles alike are all under sin. As it is written: 'There is no one righteous, not even one; there is no one who understands, no one who seeks God'" (3:9b-11). Sin is the great leveler, rendering all needy of

God's forgiveness and salvation. Given the universality of sin, all persons stand morally guilty and condemned before God, utterly incapable of redeeming themselves through righteous acts (3:19-20). But God in His grace has provided a means of salvation from this state of condemnation: Jesus Christ, by His expiatory death, redeems us from sin and justifies us before God (3:21-26). It is through Him and through Him alone, then, that God's forgiveness is available (5:12-21). To reject Jesus Christ is therefore to reject God's grace and forgiveness, to refuse the one means of salvation that God has provided. It is to remain under His condemnation and wrath, to forfeit eternal salvation. For someday God will judge all people, punishing "those who do not know God and do not obey the gospel of our Lord Jesus. They will be punished with everlasting destruction and shut out from the presence of the Lord and from the majesty of his power" (2 Thess. 1:8-9).

It wasn't just Paul who held to this exclusivist, Christocentric view of salvation. The apostle John likewise saw no salvation outside of Christ. In John's Gospel, Jesus declares, "I am the way and the truth and the life. No one comes to the Father except through me" (John 14:6). John explains that people love the darkness of sin rather than light, but that God has sent His Son into the world to save the world and to give eternal life to everyone who believes in the Son. "Whoever believes in him is not condemned, but whoever does not believe stands condemned already because he has not believed in the name of God's one and only Son" (John 3:18). People are already spiritually dead; but those who believe in Christ pass from death to life (John 5:24). In his epistles, John asserts that no one who denies the Son has the Father, and he identifies such a person as the antichrist (1 John 2:22-23; 4:3; 2 John 7). In short, "He who has the Son has life; he who does not have the Son of God does not have life" (1 John 5:12). In John's Apocalypse, it is the Lamb alone in heaven and on earth and under the earth who is worthy to open the scroll and its seven seals, for it was He that by His blood ransomed people for God from every tribe and tongue and people and nation on the earth (Rev. 5:1-14). In the consummation, everyone whose name is not found written in the Lamb's book is cast into the everlasting fire reserved for the devil and his cohorts (20:15).

One could make the same point from the other epistles in the New Testament as well. It is the conviction of the writers of the New Testament that "there is one God and one mediator between God and men, the man Christ Jesus, who gave himself as a ransom for all men" (1 Tim. 2:5-6a).

Indeed, this seems to have been the attitude of Jesus Himself. Jesus came on the scene with an unparalleled sense of divine authority, the authority to stand and speak in the place of God Himself and to call people to repentance and faith. Moreover, the object of that faith was He Himself, the absolute revelation of God: "All things have been committed to me by my Father. No one knows the Son except the Father, and no one knows the Father except the Son and those to whom the Son chooses to reveal him" (Matt. 11:27). On the Day of Judgment, a person's destiny will be determined by how he responded to Jesus: "I tell you, whoever acknowledges me before men, the Son of Man will also acknowledge him before the angels of God" (Luke 12:8). Frequent warnings concerning hell are found on Jesus' lips, and it may well be that He believed that most of mankind would be damned, whereas only a minority of mankind would be saved: "Enter through the narrow gate. For wide is the gate and broad is the road that leads to destruction, and many enter through it. But small is the gate and narrow the road that leads to life, and only a few find it" (Matt. 7:13-14). A hard teaching, no doubt; but the logic of the New Testament is simple and compelling: the universality of sin and the uniqueness of Christ's sacrifice entail that there is no salvation apart from Christ.

Although this particularity was scandalous in the polytheistic world of the first century, with the triumph of Christianity throughout the Roman Empire the scandal receded. Indeed, one of the classic marks of the church was its catholicity, and for men like Augustine and Aquinas the universality of the church was one of the signs that the Scriptures are divine revelation, since so great a structure could not have been generated by and founded upon a falsehood. Of course,

Jews remained in Christian Europe, and later the armies of Islam had to be combated, but these exceptions were hardly sufficient to overturn the catholicity of the church or to promote religious pluralism.

But with the so-called "Expansion of Europe" during the three centuries of exploration and discovery from 1450 to 1750, the situation changed radically. It was now seen that, far from being the universal religion, Christianity was confined to a small corner of the globe. This realization had a twofold impact upon people's religious thinking. First, it tended toward the relativization of religious beliefs. Since each religious system was historically and geographically limited, it seemed incredible that any of them should be regarded as universally true. It seemed that the only religion that could make a universal claim upon mankind would be a sort of general religion of nature. Second, it tended to make Christianity's claim to exclusivity appear unjustly narrow and cruel. If salvation was only through faith in Christ, then the majority of the human race was condemned to eternal damnation, since they had not so much as even heard of Christ. Again, only a natural religion available to all men seemed consistent with a fair and loving God.

In our own day the influx into Western nations of immigrants from former colonies, coupled with the advances in telecommunications that have served to shrink the world toward what Marshall McLuhan has called a "global village," has heightened both of those impressions. The impact upon Christian missions has been huge. Mainline denominations have to a great extent lost their sense of missionary calling or have been forced to reinterpret missions in terms of social engagement with peoples of the Third World, a sort of Christian Peace Corps, if you will, whereas those who continue to adhere to the traditional, orthodox view are denounced for religious intolerance. This shift is perhaps best illustrated by the attitude of the Second Vatican Council toward world mission. In its Dogmatic Constitution on the Church, the Council declared that those who have not yet received the gospel are related in various ways to the people of God. Jews, in particular, remain dear to God, but the plan of salvation also includes all who acknowledge the Creator, such as

Muslims. People who through no fault of their own do not know the gospel, but who strive to do God's will by conscience, can also be saved. The Council therefore declared in its Declaration on Non-Christian Religions that Catholics now pray *for* the Jews, not for the *conversion* of the Jews, and it also declared that the church looks with esteem upon Muslims. Missionary work seems to be directed only toward those who "serve the creature rather than the Creator" (see Rom. 1:25, RSV) or are utterly hopeless. Carefully couched in ambiguous language and often apparently internally inconsistent, the documents of Vatican II could easily be taken as a radical reinterpretation of the nature of the church and of Christian missions, according to which great numbers of non-Christians are really part of the people of God and therefore not appropriate subjects of evangelism.

In recent years certain evangelical theologians have begun to compromise on this question as well. For example, in an address to the Evangelical Theology Group at the meeting of the American Academy of Religion in San Francisco in November of 1992, Clark Pinnock declared: "I am appealing to evangelicals to make the shift to a more inclusive outlook, much the way the Catholics did at Vatican II." Pinnock expresses optimism that great numbers of the unevangelized will be saved. He says, "God will find faith in people without the person even realizing he/she had it." He even entertains the possibility of people being given another chance after death, freed from the effects of sin:

> Imagine it—People are raised from the dead by the power of Jesus' resurrection, free of whatever had obscured the love of God and prevented them from receiving it in life. . . . God is a serious lover who wants everyone with no opportunity to respond to His offer to have one. No sinner is excluded, who, having been included in salvation by God, but lacking opportunity to respond to grace [*sic*].

Pinnock realizes that his view raises the question, Doesn't this undermine both the rationale and urgency of world mission? No, says Pinnock, for:

1. God has called us to engage in mission work and we should obey. But notice that this supplies no rationale as to why God should have issued such an apparently pointless command. It just amounts to blind obedience to a command lacking any rationale.
2. Missions is broader than just securing people's eternal destiny. In other words we're back to the idea of the Christian Peace Corps.
3. Missions should be positive; it is not an ultimatum, "Believe or be damned!" Well, of course not; but it is difficult to see, with such an understanding, why the task of world mission should retain any sense of urgency. Why should I drag off my wife and children to spend fifteen of the best years of our lives struggling as missionaries in Kyrgyzstan when the people there are already saved?

I find it terribly ironic that, just as the church is on the verge of completing the task of world evangelization, it should be her own theologians who would try to trip her at the finish line!

The most radical response to our heightened awareness of the religious diversity of mankind is religious pluralism. The pluralist finds it inconceivable that any one particular religion should be true, and all the others false. So he advocates a pluralistic approach. Religious pluralism comes in two forms: what we might call unsophisticated religious pluralism, and sophisticated religious pluralism.

Unsophisticated religious pluralism responds to the phenomenon of religious diversity by saying, "They're all true! All of the world's great religions are basically saying the same thing."

Now this view, which one often hears expounded by laypeople and college sophomores, is rooted in ignorance of what the world's great religions teach. Anyone who has studied comparative religions knows that the worldviews propounded by these religions are often diametrically opposite one another. Just take Islam and Buddhism, for example. Their worldviews have almost nothing in common. Islam believes that there is a personal God who is omnipotent, omniscient, and holy, and who created the world. It believes that people are sinful and in need of God's forgiveness, that everlasting heaven or hell awaits us after death, and that we must earn our salvation by faith and righteous deeds. Buddhism denies all of these things. For the classical Buddhist ultimate reality is impersonal, the world is uncreated, there is no enduring self, life's ultimate goal is not personal immortality but annihilation, and the ideas of sin and salvation play no role at all. Examples like this could be multiplied.

Clearly all religions cannot be true. For they have contradictory views about the nature of ultimate reality, the world, man, moral values, and so on. They could all be *false,* but they cannot all be true. Unsophisticated religious pluralism is therefore untenable.

So what the sophisticated religious pluralist says is that all the world's religions are, in fact, false. None of them is true! They are all culturally relative ways of misconstruing reality. Ultimate reality, which you cannot accurately call "God," should be given some nondescript name like "the Real" or "the Absolute." Nothing can be known about it, but the world's religions all picture it in different ways. Though literally false, all the world's great religions are effective in transforming people's lives.

Sophisticated religious pluralism raises a host of questions, but I want to focus on just one: Why think that religious pluralism is true? That is to say, why can't only one, particular religion be true? What's wrong with religious particularism? Specifically, what's wrong with Christian particularism?

Well, some of the objections to Christian particularism offered by religious pluralists are just obvious logical fallacies. For example, pluralists often say that it's arrogant and immoral to claim that any one, particular religion is true. But this appears to be a textbook example of the logical fallacy philosophers call *argumentum ad hominem,* that is to say, trying to invalidate a position by attacking the character of the people who hold to it. For example, let's imagine that some medical researcher finally discovers an AIDS vaccine, and let's suppose that he is the only one to have made this discovery. But now suppose that he also happens to be an absolute jerk. He goes around bragging about his discovery and telling everyone that he has discovered the only vaccine that will ward off AIDS. He boasts that he deserves the Nobel Prize for his accomplishment. He looks down on his colleagues as mental midgets because they lacked his brilliance and ambition to discover the vaccine. He is totally arrogant and conceited. Now does his arrogance do anything at all to undermine the truth that he did discover the only AIDS vaccine? Obviously not! No one in his right mind would regard the vaccine as ineffective and refuse to take it simply because the person announcing it to the world was arrogant. The truth of the claim is independent of the character of the person making the claim. In exactly the same way, it is irrelevant to the truth of a particular religious worldview whether its adherents are arrogant or not.

In any case, why think that religious particularists must be arrogant? Suppose I've done my best to figure out which religion, if any, is true. I've read the various scriptures and attended meetings and talked with each religion's adherents and listened thoughtfully to what they've had to say. Moreover, I've prayed about my quest and sought spiritual guidance on my path. And suppose that as a result of my honest search, I'm convinced that Christianity alone is true. What else can I do but believe in it? I think it's the truth! What else am I supposed to do? If I believe in Christ because I'm convinced that his claims are true, how can I be denounced as arrogant?

In fact, this objection turns out to be a double-edged sword. For if it is arrogant and immoral to hold a religious belief that is rejected by most other people and that implies that their religious beliefs are false, then it follows that the religious pluralist himself is arrogant and immoral. For he thinks *everybody* else's religious beliefs are false, that the religious pluralist alone has seen the truth. Only religious pluralists, who are a tiny minority of mankind, are right, and everybody else is wrong. How arrogant can you get!

Another bad argument against religious particularism is that people's religious beliefs are culturally relative: for example, if you had been born in Pakistan, you would likely be a Muslim; but if you had been born in Ireland, you'd more likely have been at least nominally a Catholic. Therefore, none of these particular religious beliefs can be true.

This argument is a textbook example of the logical fallacy that philosophers call the genetic fallacy. This is trying to invalidate a view by showing how a person came to hold that view. Such a move is obviously fallacious. For example, as a twenty-first-century Westerner you believe that the earth is roughly spherical and orbits the sun. But if you had been born in ancient Greece, you would have likely believed that the sun orbits the earth, and maybe even that the earth is flat. So does that mean that your belief that the earth goes around the sun or that the earth is round is therefore false, or unjustified? Obviously not!

And this argument, too, turns out to be a double-edged sword. For if the religious pluralist had been born in Pakistan or Spain, then he would likely have been a religious particularist! So by his own argument, his religious pluralism is false. His believing it is just the accidental result of his being born in late twentieth-century, politically correct, Western society!

Now please don't think that, just because such fallacious arguments are often given on behalf of religious pluralism, pluralism does not pose a serious challenge to Christian belief. On the contrary, I think that it does. But clearing away these fallacious arguments can help us to get to the real problem lurking in the background. That problem concerns the fate of unbelievers outside of one's particular religious tradition. That problem is especially poignant for Christians, who believe that salvation from sin and eternal life are to be found only through Christ's atoning death on the cross. Given the universality of sin and the uniqueness of Christ's substitutionary death on our behalf, it follows that salvation is found only through Christ. But religious pluralists find this unconscionable.

Nowhere is this better illustrated than in the life of my own doctoral mentor John Hick. Hick began his career as a relatively conservative Christian theologian. His first book was entitled *Christianity at the Centre*.[1] But as Hick began to study the other world religions and to become acquainted with many of their saintly adherents, he found it simply inconceivable that such good people should be on their way

---

[1] John Hick, *Christianity at the Centre* (London: SCM, 1968).

to hell. But he realized what that meant. Somehow he had to get Jesus Christ out of the center. So long as Christ's incarnation and atoning death were preserved, Christ could not be successfully marginalized. Hick therefore came to produce a book entitled *The Myth of God Incarnate,* in which he argues that these central Christian doctrines are not true but mere myths. He wrote:

> For understood literally, the Son of God, God the Son, God-incarnate language implies that God can be adequately known and responded to only through Jesus; and the whole religious life of mankind, beyond the stream of Judaic-Christian faith is thus by implication excluded as lying outside the sphere of salvation. This implication did little positive harm so long as Christendom was a largely autonomous civilization with only relatively marginal interaction with the rest of mankind. But with the clash between the Christian and Muslim worlds, and then on an ever broadening front with European colonization throughout the earth, the literal understanding of the mythological language of Christian disciple-ship has had a divisive effect upon the relations between that minority of human beings who live within the borders of the Christian tradition and that majority who live outside it and within other streams of religious life.
>
> 　Transposed into theological terms, the problem which has come to the surface in the encounter of Christianity with the other world religions is this: If Jesus was literally God incarnate, and if it is by his death alone that men can be saved, and by their response to him alone that they can appropriate that salvation, then the only door-way to eternal life is Christian faith. It would follow from this that the large majority of the human race so far have not been saved. But is it credible that the loving God and Father of all men has decreed that only those born within one particular thread of human history shall be saved?[2]

This is the real problem raised by the religious diversity of mankind: the fate of those who stand outside one's own particular religious tradition.

---

[2] John Hick, "Jesus and the World Religions," in John Hick, ed., *The Myth of God Incarnate* (London: SCM, 1977), 179-180.

But what exactly is the problem supposed to be here? What's wrong with saying that salvation is to be found through Christ alone?

Is the problem supposed to be simply the idea that a loving God wouldn't send people to hell? Is that what the problem is? Well, I don't think so. The Bible says that God desires all men to be saved and to come to a knowledge of the truth (1 Tim. 2:4; 2 Pet. 3:9). Therefore, through the work of the Holy Spirit, God draws all men to Himself, seeking to convict them of sin and bring them to repentance. Anybody who makes a free and well-informed decision to reject Christ thus seals his own fate; he is self-condemned. His damnation can't be blamed on God: on the contrary, he has resisted God's every effort to save him. He separates himself from God forever, in defiance of God's will that he be saved. In a sense, then, God doesn't send anybody to hell—people send themselves.

Is the problem then supposed to be that a loving God wouldn't send people to hell if they are uninformed or misinformed about Christ? Is that what the problem is supposed to be? Well, again, that doesn't seem to be the heart of the problem. God is fair, and according to Romans 1 and 2, God doesn't judge people who haven't heard about Christ by the same standard as those who have. It would be manifestly unfair to condemn people for not believing in Christ when they've never heard of Christ. Rather, God judges them on the basis of the information that they do have, as God has revealed it to all mankind in nature and conscience. Theologians call this God's general revelation, and it is by their response to its light that people without the gospel will be judged. According to Paul, all mankind can know through nature that a Creator God exists, and they can know through their own conscience God's moral law and their failure to live up to it. Simply on the basis of nature and conscience, then, all people everywhere should recognize their guilt before God and repent, seeking His mercy and forgiveness.

Unfortunately, it is the sad testimony of Scripture that people don't even live up to this standard. They ignore the Creator and worship gods of their own making, and they flout the moral law, immersing themselves in immorality. Therefore, even when judged by standards much lower than those revealed in the gospel, the mass of humanity stands condemned before God. Oh, it's conceivable that a few might recognize God and His moral law and turn to Him in repentance and faith and that God might accordingly apply to them the benefits of Christ's blood so that they might be saved without a conscious knowledge of Christ. They would be like certain Old Testament figures like Job and Melchizedek, who had no conscious knowledge of Christ and, indeed, were not even Israelites or members of the old covenant, but who nevertheless enjoyed a saving relationship with God in virtue of Christ's atoning death. So even where the message of Christ is yet unknown, salvation is universally accessible to anyone at any time through a faith response to God's general revelation in nature and conscience. But if we take Scripture seriously, then it's evident that very few people actually access salvation in this way. Most people freely turn their backs on God's general revelation in nature and conscience.

Rather the real problem posed by religious particularism seems to me to be this: if God is all-knowing, as the Bible declares Him to be, then even prior to His creation of the world, God must have known who would receive Christ and be saved and who would not. But if this is the case, then certain difficult questions arise:

1. Why didn't God bring the gospel to people who reject the light of general revelation that they have, but who would have believed if only they had heard the gospel?

2. More fundamentally, why did God even create the world at all, if He knew that so many people would not receive Christ and would therefore be lost?

3. Even more radically, why didn't God create a world in which He knew everyone would freely receive Christ and be saved?

These are hard questions! How is the Christian supposed to reply? Does Christianity make God out to be cruel and unloving?

In order to answer these questions, we need to probe more deeply into the logic of the problem before us. Basically, what the pluralist is saying is that it is impossible for God to be all-powerful and all-good and yet for some people never to hear the gospel and to therefore be lost. He's saying that if God really has those attributes, then anybody and everybody who exists must be saved.

But why is this the case? After all, there's no explicit contradiction between the statements "God is all-powerful and all-loving" and "Some people never hear the gospel and are therefore lost." If the pluralist is saying that these statements are *implicitly* contradictory, then he must be assuming some hidden premises that would bring out the contradiction and make it explicit. Let's try to ferret out these assumptions. It seems to me that they are two in number:

(i) If God is all-powerful, He can create a world in which everybody hears the gospel and is freely saved.
(ii) If God is all-loving, He prefers a world in which everybody hears the gospel and is freely saved.

Given the necessary truth of (i) and (ii), says the pluralist, it follows from God's being all-powerful and all-loving that everyone must hear the gospel and be freely saved, which is incompatible with Christian particularism.

Now in order for the pluralist's reasoning to be sound, both of these hidden premises must be necessarily true. But are they? Let's see.

Let's look at the first assumption, that *If God is all-powerful, He can create a world in which everybody hears the gospel and is freely saved.* I think we can agree that God could create a world in which everybody hears the gospel. But so long as creatures are genuinely free, it is by no means clear that He can bring it about that everybody would freely believe in the gospel and be saved. Being all-powerful does not mean being able to do logical impossibilities, like make a round triangle or a married bachelor. Indeed, such contradictory combinations of words don't really describe any things at all. It is logically impossible to *make* someone *freely* do something. For being made to do an action by someone else is logically inconsistent with your doing the action freely. To do an action freely just means that you do it without anyone else's making you do it. Therefore, so long as people are free, there's no guarantee that in a world in which everybody heard the gospel, everybody would be freely saved. In fact, when you think about it, there's no guarantee that in such a world the balance between saved and lost would be any better than the balance in the actual world! It's possible that in any world of free creatures which God could create, some people would freely reject Him and be lost.

So it seems that the first assumption is just not necessarily true. It may not be within God's power to create a world in which everyone hears the gospel and is freely saved. The pluralist's argument is therefore invalid.

But what about that second assumption, that *If God is all-loving, He prefers a world in which everybody hears the gospel and is saved* over a world in which some people are lost? Is that assumption necessarily true? Let's concede for the sake of argument that the first assumption is true: there are possible worlds that God could create in which everyone hears the gospel and freely accepts it. Does God's being all-loving compel Him to prefer one of these worlds to the actual world? Not necessarily. For these worlds might have other, overriding deficiencies that make them less preferable. For example, suppose the only worlds in which everybody hears and freely believes the gospel are worlds with only a handful of people in them, say, three or four. If God created any more people, then at least one of them would not believe and so would be lost. Now I ask you: does God's being all-loving compel Him to prefer one of these radically underpopulated worlds over a world in which multitudes freely receive Christ and are saved, though some others freely reject Christ? That's not at all obvious to me! Why should the joy and blessedness of those who would freely receive Christ be precluded by some other people who would freely spurn God's love and forgiveness? So long as God offers sufficient grace for salvation to all people, I don't see that He is any less loving for preferring a more populous world, even though that means some people would freely reject Him and His every effort to save them and therefore would be lost.

So neither of the crucial assumptions made by our objector is necessarily true. God's being all-powerful doesn't guarantee that He can create a world in which everybody freely receives Christ, nor does God's being all-loving compel Him to prefer a world in which everybody is saved over a world in which some are lost. If either one of these assumptions is not necessarily true, then the pluralist's whole argument is invalid. Since both of these assumptions fail, the pluralist's case is doubly invalid.

But we can even go one step further than this. We can actually prove that it's entirely consistent to believe that God is all-powerful and all-loving and that some people never hear the gospel and are therefore lost.

To begin with, since He is good and loving, God wants as many people as possible to be saved and as few people as possible to be lost. His goal, then, is to create no more of the lost than is necessary to achieve a certain number of the saved. In other words, God wants heaven to be as full as possible and hell to be as empty as possible, and He needs to find the optimal balance between these.

But it's possible that the actual world has such a balance! It's possible that in order to create this many people who will be saved, God also had to create this many people who will be lost. It's possible that had God created a world in which fewer people go to hell, then even fewer people proportionately would have gone to heaven. It's possible that in order to achieve a multitude of saints, God had to accept a multitude of sinners.

It might be objected, however, that an all-good God would not create persons who He knew would be lost as a by-product of His creating persons who He knew would be saved. But this objection misconstrues my proposal. It is true that the existence of lost people is an undesired concomitant of a world having people who freely receive God's grace and are saved. But that does not imply that God's plan of salvation does not include those who freely reject it and are lost. Remember, God loves everyone He creates and gives sufficient grace for salvation to each one of them. Indeed, some of the lost may actually receive greater grace than some of the saved. The lost are not created as mere means to some end, say, the salvation of the elect. Rather as persons created in God's image the lost are ends in themselves and are loved and valued by God, who wills their salvation and strives to achieve it. But of their own free will some people reject God's loving initiatives and are lost. It remains God's will and desire that all mankind, including those who finally separate themselves from God forever, be saved and come to the knowledge of the truth.

But someone might further object that God would not create persons who He knew will be lost but who would have been saved if only they had heard the gospel. But how do we know that there are such persons? It's reasonable to assume that many people who never hear the gospel would not have believed the gospel even if they had heard it. After all, not everybody believes in the gospel and is saved when missionaries finally succeed in bringing the Good News to some previously unreached people group. Thus, it's reasonable to think that at least some people who never hear the gospel and are lost would not have believed in it even if they had heard it. Suppose, then, that God has so providentially ordered the world that *all* persons who never hear the gospel are precisely such people. In that case, anybody who never hears the gospel and is lost would have rejected the gospel and been lost even if he had heard it. No one could stand before God on the Judgement Day and complain, "Sure, God, I didn't respond to your revelation in nature and conscience, but if only I had heard the gospel, then I would have believed!" God would say, "No, I knew that even if you had heard the gospel, you wouldn't have believed it. Therefore, my judgement of you on the basis of nature and conscience is neither unfair nor unloving."

Thus, it's possible that God has created a world which has an optimal balance between saved and lost and that those who never hear the gospel and are therefore lost would not have believed in Christ even if they had heard of Him. So long as this scenario is even *possible,* it proves that there is no incompatibility between an all-powerful, all-loving God and some people's not hearing the gospel and thus being lost.

Now let me head off a possible misunderstanding at this point. Somebody might say, "Well, why engage in missionary work, then, if all the people who are unreached would not receive Christ even if they heard of Him?" The question forgets that we're talking only about people who *never* hear the gospel. God in His providence can so arrange the world that as the gospel spreads out from first-century Palestine, He places people in its path who would believe it if they heard it. In His love and mercy, God ensures that no one who would believe the gospel if he heard it remains ultimately unreached. Once the gospel reaches a people group, God providentially places there persons who He knew would respond to it if they heard it. He ensures that those who *never* hear it are only people who wouldn't accept it even if they did hear it.

So now we're ready to provide possible answers to the three difficult questions that prompted our discussion. Let's take them in reverse order:

1. *Why didn't God create a world in which He knew everyone would freely receive Christ and be saved?* Answer: It may not be within God's power to create such a world. If such a world were feasible, God would have created it. But given His will to create free creatures, God had to accept the fact that some would reject Him and be lost.

2. *Why did God create the world, if He knew that so many people would not receive Christ and would therefore be lost?* Answer: God wanted to share His love and fellowship with created persons. This constitutes an incommensurable good for human beings. God knew that this meant that many would freely reject Him and be lost. But the blessedness and happiness of those who would accept Him should not be precluded by those who would freely reject Him. Those who would willingly reject God and forfeit salvation should not be allowed to have a sort of "veto power" over which worlds God is free to create. But God in His loving-kindness has providentially ordered the world to achieve an optimal balance between the saved and the lost by maximizing the number of those who accept Him and minimizing the number of those who do not.

3. *Why didn't God bring the gospel to people who reject the light of general revelation that they have, but who would have believed if only they had heard the gospel?* Answer: There are no such people. God in His providence

has so arranged the world that those who would respond to the gospel if they heard it are born at a time and place in history where they do hear it. Those who do not respond to God's revelation in nature and conscience and never hear the gospel would not have responded to it even if they did hear it. Hence, no one is lost because of a lack of information or due to historical or geographical accident. Anyone who wants—or even would want—to be saved will be saved.

These are only possible answers to the difficult questions we set for ourselves. Are they true answers? Only God knows! The important point to be grasped here is that so long as the scenario we have constructed is even possible, it proves that there is no incompatibility between God's being all-powerful and all-loving and some people's not hearing the gospel and thus being lost.

But before we conclude, I want to add that one of the attractions of the proposed scenario for me is that it does seem quite biblical as well. In his open-air address to the Athenian philosophers gathered on the Areopagus, Paul declared:

> The God who made the world and everything in it is the Lord of heaven and earth and . . . gives all men life and breath and everything else. From one man he made every nation of men, that they should inhabit the whole earth; and he determined the times set for them and the exact places where they should live. God did this so that men would seek him and perhaps reach out for him and find him, though he is not far from each one of us. "For in him we live and move and have our being" (Acts 17:24-28a).

Paul's description of God's providential arrangement of the world's peoples with a view toward their reaching out and finding God is remarkably in line with the conclusion I have reached through philosophical reflection alone.

Now the pluralist might concede the logical compatibility of God's being all-powerful and all-loving and some people's never hearing the gospel and thus being lost, but insist that the scenario I have envisioned is nonetheless very improbable. For people by and large seem to believe in the religion of the culture in which they were raised. But in that case, the pluralist may argue, it is highly probable that if many of those who never hear the gospel had been raised in a Christian culture, they would have believed the gospel and would have been saved. Thus, the hypothesis I have offered is highly implausible.

It would, indeed, be fantastically improbable that by happenstance alone it just turns out that all those who never hear the gospel and are therefore lost are persons who would not have believed the gospel even if they had heard it. But that's not the hypothesis! The hypothesis is that a provident God has so arranged the world. Given an all-knowing God who knows how every person would freely respond to His grace in whatever circumstances God might place him, it is not at all implausible that God has ordered the world in the way described. Such a world wouldn't look outwardly any different from a world in which the circumstances of a person's birth are a matter of happenstance. We can agree that people generally adopt the religion of their culture and that if many of those born into non-Christian cultures had been born in a Christian society instead, they would have been culturally Christian. But that's not to say that they would have been saved. The pluralist might insist that such a world as I envision would look significantly different than the actual world. He might claim that persons who would have been merely cultural Christians (had they been born in a Christian society) would look different somehow from persons who would have become regenerate Christians. But this claim is manifestly untrue. It is a simple empirical fact that there are no distinguishing psychological or sociological traits between persons who become Christians and persons who are nonbelievers. There is no way to predict accurately by examining a person whether and under what circumstances that person would believe in Christ for salvation. Since a world providentially ordered by God would appear outwardly identical to a world in which one's birth is a matter of historical and geographical accident, it's hard to see how the hypothesis I have defended can be deemed to be improbable.

Some people might be troubled that such a scenario sounds dis-
turbingly Euro-centric and racist, implying that white Westerners are
the good believers while all the people of the Third World are hardened infidels. But apart from its philosophical problems,[3] such a mis-
giving betrays an ignorance of contemporary demographics. Recall
the statistics presented in chapter 5 on the growth of evangelical
Christianity over the ages. Today evangelical Christianity is growing
at a rate over three times faster than the world's population. In the
Third World evangelical Christianity is undergoing an explosive
increase. Did you realize that in 1987 the number of evangelicals in
Asia surpassed the number of evangelicals in North America? Did
you realize that just four years later in 1991 the number of evangelicals in Asia surpassed the number of evangelicals *in the entire Western
World?* Christianity is not a Western, white man's religion. Today two-
thirds of evangelicals live in the Third World. Moreover, do you realize that most of the people who have ever lived on the face of this
planet are alive *right now,* at this very moment? When you reflect on
the fact that what philosophers call "the actual world" includes not
only all of the past and the present but all of the future as well, then
the problem of the unevangelized may be seen in its true perspective.
As time goes on, the percentage of the human race who never heard
the gospel will dwindle to a small fraction, while those who embrace
the gospel will, Lord willing, grow and grow until it comprises a great
multitude "from every tribe and tongue and people and nation" (Rev.
5:9), of which Caucasians are but a minority.

In conclusion, then, it seems that the presence of other world religions does not undermine the Christian gospel of salvation through
Christ alone. On the contrary, what we've said helps to put the proper

---

[3] The objector has a flawed anthropology: he thinks a person is identical to his body. But given the
biblical anthropology of body-soul dualism, one's particular body is an accidental feature of one's
being. The same soul could have been instantiated in a Caucasoid, Negroid, or Mongoloid body.
Thus, one's race or ethnicity is not an essential feature of one's identity (which is one reason why
racism is so stupid, we being all essentially similar). So if God knew that a person would not have
received Christ were he a twelfth-century Incan, but would have done so were he a twentieth-
century Nigerian, that would give God reason to create that person as the Nigerian rather than as
the Incan. Today God may be providentially placing those who would believe in the Third World
rather than in Europe!

perspective on Christian missions: it is our duty to proclaim the gospel to the whole world, trusting that God has so providentially ordered things that through us the Good News will come to persons who God knew would accept it if they heard it. There are literally divine appointments out there waiting for you. Our compassion toward those in other world religions is expressed, not in pretending they are not lost and dying without Christ, but by supporting and making every effort ourselves to communicate to them the life-giving message of the gospel of Christ.

GENERAL INDEX

SCRIPTURE INDEX

1 Corinthians
6:9-10   136
8:1b-3   40
14:20   26

2 Corinthians
2:11   35
4:16-18   99
6:4-5   99
12:9a   53
12:9b-10   53-54

Galatians
6:17   98

Ephesians
2:12   145
5:32   137
6:12   33

Colossians
2:2   36
2:8   35

1 Thessalonians
1:5   36

2 Thessalonians
1:8-9   146

1 Timothy
2:5-6a   147

James
1:6-8   48
4:3   47

1 Peter
5:8   34

1 John
2:20, 27   36
3:21-22   56
5:7-10a   36
5:12   146
5:14-15   53

Revelation
5:9   164
21:4   100